THE ENGLISH
REFORMATION

THE ENGLISH REFORMATION

A very brief history

ALEC RYRIE

First published in Great Britain in 2020

Society for Promoting Christian Knowledge
36 Causton Street
London SW1P 4ST
www.spck.org.uk

British Library Cataloguing-in-Publication Data
A catalogue record for this book is available from the British Library

ISBN 978–0–281–08240–7
eBook ISBN 978–0–281–07653–6

1 3 5 7 9 10 8 6 4 2

Typeset by Manila Typesetting Company

eBook by Manila Typesetting Company

Produced on paper from sustainable forests

For Peter Marshall

Contents

Chronology

1545	Council of Trent (Trento) assembles
1546	Execution of Anne Askew
1547	Death of Henry VIII, accession of Edward VI
1547–8	Dissolution of the chantries
1549	First Book of Common Prayer
	Rebellions across England
	Fall of Protector Somerset
1552	Second Book of Common Prayer
1553	Death of Edward VI
	Brief 'reign' of Jane Grey
	Accession of Mary I
1554	Mary marries Philip of Spain
	England restored to papal obedience
1555	Heresy executions begin
1558	Death of Mary I and Cardinal Pole, accession of Elizabeth I
1559	'Elizabethan Settlement' and revised Book of Common Prayer
1559–60	Reformation-rebellion in Scotland
1560	Geneva Bible
1563	First edition of Foxe's 'Book of Martyrs'
1568	Mary, Queen of Scots imprisoned in England
	Catholic seminary founded at Douai
1569–70	Rebellion of the northern earls and consequent reprisals
1570	Elizabeth I excommunicated
1573	Execution of papal loyalists resumes
1577	Archbishop Grindal defies Elizabeth I and placed under house arrest
1581	'Brownist' or separatist church in the Netherlands

1585	Open English military intervention in the Netherlands begins war with Spain
1586	Babington Plot and trial of Mary, Queen of Scots
1587	Execution of Mary, Queen of Scots
1588	Martin Marprelate tracts
	Spanish Armada
1594	First edition of Hooker's *Laws of Ecclesiastical Polity*
1593–1603	Nine Years' War in Ireland
1603	Death of Elizabeth I, accession of James I (James VI of Scots)
1605	Gunpowder Plot
1607	First Church of England church outside the British Isles, at Jamestown, Virginia
1611	King James Bible
1612	Last burnings for heresy in England
1620	Puritan settlement in Massachusetts
1625	Death of James I, accession of Charles I
1633	William Laud appointed Archbishop of Canterbury
1637	Prayer Book rebellion in Scotland
	Scottish National Covenant
1639–40	'Bishops' Wars' with Scottish Covenanters
1640	'Long Parliament' summoned
1641	Rebellion in Ireland
1642–6	First Civil War in England
1646	Westminster Confession
1648	Second Civil War
	New Model Army purges Parliament
1649	Execution of Charles I, declaration of a British republic

1651	Charles II crowned king of Scots, expelled after English invasion
1653–8	Oliver Cromwell is Lord Protector
1656	Readmission of Jews to England
1660	Restoration of Charles II
1662	Revised Book of Common Prayer
1678–81	'Popish Plot'
1688–9	'Glorious Revolution'
	Act of Toleration
1701	Act of Settlement bars Catholics from the throne
1707	Act of Union between England and Scotland
1780	Anti-Catholic Gordon Riots in London
1784	Samuel Seabury consecrated as presiding bishop of the Protestant Episcopal Church of the USA
1791	US Bill of Rights prohibits establishment of religion
1801	Act of Union between Britain and Ireland
1829	Catholic Emancipation
1850	Catholic hierarchy restored in Britain
1871	Disestablishment of the (Anglican) Church of Ireland
1919	Church Assembly created in England
1920	Disestablishment of the Church in Wales
1928	Revisions to the Book of Common Prayer blocked in Parliament
1994	First women ordained as priests in the Church of England
2007	British prime ministers withdraw from appointing Anglican bishops
2014	Women bishops in the Church of England legalized

Introduction

There is no such thing as 'the English Reformation'. A 'Reformation' is a composite event which is only made visible by being framed in the right way. It is like a 'war': a label we put on to a particular set of events, while we decide that other – equally violent – acts are not part of that or of any 'war'. Sixteenth- and seventeenth-century English people knew that they were living through an age of religious upheaval, but they did not know that it was 'the English Reformation', any more than the soldiers at the battle of Agincourt knew that they were fighting in 'the Hundred Years' War'.

The bare outline of the events we call 'the English Reformation' is straightforward enough. It is a story unavoidably dominated by successive kings and queens. During the reign of Henry VIII (1509–47), England broke away from the papacy and embraced some aspects of the Protestant Reformation that was unfolding on the Continent. During the short reign of his son Edward VI (1547–53), the country moved in a much more decisively Protestant direction. That was promptly reversed by the Catholic restoration under Queen Mary (1553–8), which was itself overturned by a Protestant restoration under Queen Elizabeth (1558–1603). Not least because of Elizabeth's longevity, her idiosyncratic Protestant 'settlement' stuck. Versions of it were maintained by her successors James I (1603–25) and Charles I (1625–49) – at least until civil war swept King Charles from power, cost him his head, and pitched England's religious life into turmoil once again.

But what does this story mean? Plainly these religious upheavals permanently changed England and, by extension, the many other countries on which English culture has made its mark. There is not, however, a single master narrative of all this turmoil. How could there be? It was played out at every level of an increasingly diverse society, as highly visible political changes and shifts in public religion shaped, and were shaped by, the lives of millions of people. The way you choose to tell the story is governed by what you think is important and what is trivial, by whether there are heroes or villains you want to celebrate or condemn, and by the legacies and lessons which you think matter. Once you have chosen your frame, it will give you the story you want.

So this book does not tell 'the story' of 'the English Reformation'. It tells the stories of six English Reformations or, rather, six stories of religious change in sixteenth- and seventeenth-century England. The stories are parallel and overlapping, but each has a somewhat different chronological frame, cast of characters and set of pivotal events, and has left a different legacy.

Which, if any, of these stories is true? 'Truth' is a gold standard. Historians prefer to deal in 'facts', a paper currency whose value is always open to question. Certainly none of these stories is the whole truth. They are, rather, as close to tolerably accurate as this historian's craft can make it. Which of them you prefer is up to you. As for me, I hope my own preferences are not too plain: apart from my enduring dislike of foisting our own narratives on to people who cannot now gainsay us but were once as passionate, intelligent, foolish, ignorant and alive as we are.

1

Catholic Reformation

Christianity first came to the country we now call England in Roman times. In the sixteenth century, the age of the Reformation, not everyone believed the legend that Joseph of Arimathea had brought the gospel to Britannia in the first century, and planted a thorn on Glastonbury Tor; but the equally legendary tale of how Pope Eleutherius had converted King Lucius of the Britons to Christianity in the second century was common knowledge. Moreover, Constantine, the first Christian Roman emperor, was claimed as an honorary Briton on the basis that he had begun his reign in York. Still, all this was only prelude. The collapse of Roman rule and a wave of pagan Anglo-Saxon settlement in the fifth century pushed Romano-British Christianity to the island's western fringes, and above all to Ireland. The incomers had to be converted afresh. In the year 597 a far from legendary missionary named Augustine, sent by the equally real Pope Gregory the Great, persuaded King Ethelbert of Kent that he and his kingdom ought to become Christian. Augustine became England's first archbishop at Canterbury, Ethelbert's capital. His successors down to the present have sat on his throne.

Sixteenth-century English Christians could therefore look back on nearly a millennium of unbroken history. And whether they thanked Eleutherius or Gregory, they could take particular pride in being the first nation to be converted at the hands of a pope. For a country at almost the farthest edge of Christendom, this connection to the Apostolic See of Rome was a point of pride. A cynic might say that it cost England very little to be ostentatiously loyal to the pope, since Rome was too far away to make much of a nuisance of itself – but equally, this meant that England's voice was under-represented in the Church's councils. There has as yet been only one English pope (Adrian IV, 1154–9), although as we will see, in the sixteenth century there were a couple of near misses.

Nevertheless, a strong Anglo-papal axis was a recurring fact of medieval English life. Duke William of Normandy legitimized his conquest of England in 1066 with a papal endorsement. King Henry II was made lord of Ireland by a grant of that sole English pope in 1155. King John, who was the closest medieval England came to having an antipapal ruler, had by the end of his reign reversed his position so dramatically that he formally granted sovereignty over the entire realm to Pope Innocent III. During the great schism of 1378–1417, England was stoutly loyal to the popes in Rome, rejecting the rival claimants in Avignon. In 1485, Pope Innocent VIII gave the newly and precariously crowned Henry VII a much-needed endorsement by accepting his tenuous claims to the English throne and permitting him to marry his royal cousin, Elizabeth of York. King Henry, an invariably sharp-eyed propagandist, had the papal bull translated into English and printed for general circulation. The logic was the same as it had been for centuries. Kings and popes both had far more to gain from working together than they ever could from confrontation.

This long history has helped to foster the myth of the Middle Ages as an undifferentiated 'Age of Faith', whether depicted as an Eden of Catholic innocence or as a thousand years of Babylonian captivity. Of course this is not so. Neither in England nor elsewhere in Europe could Catholic Christendom have flourished for so long by remaining static. The Catholic world's astonishing durability testifies to its power to reinvent itself. Throughout the Middle Ages, established patterns of religious life were challenged by movements of 'reform' – some consciously led from Rome, but many more bubbling up as local initiatives, often in the form of new or reformed orders of monks, nuns, friars or canons. The Church's hierarchy suppressed or even persecuted initiatives which posed an unacceptable challenge, but it much preferred, where it could, to tolerate, tame or co-opt them. They were its engine of renewal.

If there was a single pattern to these myriad reforming initiatives, it was a cycle in which formality, laxity, habit and corruption was periodically challenged by new or revived movements of invigorated discipline and holiness. For example, in the early thirteenth century the Franciscan friars brought a newly austere approach to the discipline of poverty. They then settled into less rigorous patterns of living, only to be challenged afresh from within their own ranks by a so-called 'Observant' movement which sprang up to oppose this laxity, and was formalized in the fifteenth century. Henry VII, with his sharp eye for branding opportunities, made himself patron of a new English province of the Observants.

This cycle of holiness and laxity was, however, a spiral, not a circle. With each turn, its scope widened from the clerical and monastic elite to the population at large. The Franciscans, unlike their monastic predecessors, set out to live among and minister to the common people. Some fourteenth- and fifteenth-century innovations abandoned formal religious orders altogether, allowing lay men and women to live in quasi-monastic communities, sometimes only temporarily rather than as a lifelong vocation. The slow spread of literacy, accelerated by the development of printing in the mid-fifteenth century, symbolized a change in how lay Christians related to their Church. No longer simply the passive consumers of its sacramental services and the subjects of its prayers, they were participating. Books of hours, written so that lay people could pray as monks did within the fabric of their everyday lives, became a staple of the late medieval book trade.

So the English Church in the early sixteenth century was hungry for reform, but that was neither an unusual nor an alarming condition. Loyal and earnestly pious churchmen were painfully aware that the English Church fell short of its high ideals – even though, compared realistically both to its own past and to the rest of Latin Christendom, it was in pretty good shape. Its clergy were better disciplined and educated, and its parishes better equipped, than ever before. Its lay people – many of them – were hungry to be brought deeper into the Church's life, and it was being done. The plainest sign of success in England was that a dissident movement offering more radical lay empowerment, the diffuse sect known as the 'Lollards', never won any kind of mass following after its brief flowering in the late fourteenth century.

But for the Church's most ambitious leaders, 'good enough' was not good enough, and modest successes only underlined how much more there was to be done. By the early sixteenth century, this long-standing unease had begun to merge with a new movement for reform that was sweeping Christendom and which put down particularly deep roots in England. 'Christian humanism', as historians call it, was the latest turn of the medieval spiral of reform: an attempt to apply the methods and insights of the Renaissance to religious life. Its most important prophet, the sharp-tongued, peripatetic Dutch monk Desiderius Erasmus, spent some years in England and inspired a generation of English scholars. His closest English friend, Thomas More, won a Continent-wide reputation in his own right. Fittingly enough, More was a layman, not a priest, and his teasing vision of an ideal society in *Utopia* (1516) summed up the Christian humanists' dreams. In this imagined land, the actual priests were very few and very holy, but the entire population lived in such simplicity and purity that the island of Utopia amounted to a giant monastery. They prized learning, justice and charity over rites and superstitions. In Utopia, the spiral of reform had reached its limit, and had included everyone. The book's opening chapters made explicit the contrast with More's home island, where the rich and powerful claimed to be Christians but had forgotten peace, mercy and the needs of the poor.

Utopia was a satire, but the Christian humanists did more than offer impossible counsels of perfection from the sidelines. More himself reluctantly entered King Henry VIII's service, and paid dearly for it. Another far more compromised but far more powerful reformer was already pressing this agenda forward. Cardinal-Archbishop Thomas Wolsey, whose administrative omnicompetence made him effective ruler of England on Henry VIII's behalf from *c.* 1514 to 1529, has been remembered more for ambition and corruption than for reform and idealism. Yet this was a man who turned a narcissistic, warmongering king's diplomatic difficulties into a hard-nosed scheme for universal, perpetual peace between the European powers, with England and the papacy acting as the guarantors. The failure of this impossible project is hardly surprising. What is astonishing is that Wolsey secured such wide international agreement to it, and that for a few mirage-like months it seemed to be working. In this context, his own perfectly realistic ambitions to be elected pope look less ignoble.

England was in the end too weak a power, and Henry VIII too capricious a king, for Wolsey to use them to leverage humanist dreams into existence. But there was nothing to stop his ambition, cunning and idealism from reshaping his own country. If England's Catholic Reformation had a start date, it was 1518, when Wolsey was made a papal legate with sweeping powers to reshape the English Church. It was almost the first time that England's Church, divided as it was between the two provinces of Canterbury and York, had been treated as a single entity. The flagship project Wolsey launched with these new powers was a sign of what might be to come. A huge amount of the English Church's considerable wealth was tied up in monastic houses: communities whose cloistered piety was of course laudable, but was several turns of the spiral behind the times. Moreover, not all of the monks fully lived up to their orders' ideals. Wolsey used his new powers to close down a swathe of problematic or inconvenient houses, redirecting the funds to a much more fashionably pious purpose: education. A splendid new school in his home town of Ipswich would feed into a splendid new college at his old university of Oxford.

Wolsey's project manager for this tricky enterprise was another compromised Catholic reformer. What made Thomas Cromwell stand out from London's crowd of ambitious jobbing lawyers was his years spent in Italy as a soldier, merchant and all-purpose man on the make. That had given him the contacts to find the Italian sculptors and artists Wolsey wanted to employ, but Cromwell had picked up more in Italy than an ear for languages and an eye for marble. Like many northern Europeans who visited Rome at the height of the Renaissance papacy's decadence, he left with a hunch that the pope was part of the problem, not part of the solution, and that the cutting edge of the spiral of reform was now a long way from the old centre. It also gave him a very Italian sense of what reform might mean.

The Italian Reformation is a story now so thoroughly forgotten that the phrase sounds like a contradiction, but during the 1520s and 1530s it seemed like a real possibility. Much of the structure of the Church in Italy was corrupt or dysfunctional, so reformers worked around it, creating new orders and fraternities which explored patterns of simplified piety. In Germany, when a dispute about the doctrine of salvation triggered by a friar called Martin Luther flared up in 1517–18, it quickly turned into a slanging match in which all the talk was of obedience, submission and heresy. In Italy, however, idealistic, loyal churchmen were keen to do with Luther what had been done with so many other disruptive reformers over the centuries: absorb, co-opt and housetrain his insights, views which pushed Catholic orthodoxy in a particular direction but did not, yet, contradict it.

The 'Reformation' which Italy's so-called *spirituali* championed did not come to pass. The increasingly bitter confrontation with Luther's movement forced the Catholic world away from creative compromises. But we can easily imagine that, had Tudor marriage politics not intervened, it is the kind of Reformation that England would have had. If

England had held on to its thousand-year tradition of loyal papalism, the result would not have been a simple extension of the medieval Church, frozen in time. In that alternative history, England's monasteries would not have been suppressed systematically as they were in the 1530s, but nor would they have sailed on into the modern era untouched. Eager Catholic reformers, keen to build a nation of earnest believers and wary of the formalism and superstition that accreted around monastic life, would have continued where Wolsey and Cromwell had begun, systematically redirecting the monasteries' enormous wealth to more modish purposes like education, missionary work and the relief of the poor. In a century of rapid economic change, with populations rising, wages falling and landowners driving their tenants off the land and into destitution, a reforming Catholic Church would have pushed back against this new economy and its consequences, although probably with more zeal than effect. Defending the 'commonwealth' against depredations such as the enclosure of land and the blocking of rivers with fish-weirs became a Protestant cause in the 1540s and 1550s, but there is no doctrinal reason why it should have been so. Reforming Catholic bishops such as Erasmus' friend Cuthbert Tunstall, Bishop of London and Durham, found this moral case as compelling as did evangelicals like Thomas Cromwell.

This is not history, but imagination. Still, there are at least two, linked reasons to treat the fantasy seriously. One is named Reginald Pole. Pole was a man to conjure with: a young cousin of Henry VIII whose family had a dangerously strong claim to the throne in their own right, and whose decision to spend the early 1530s studying in Italy was political as well as academic. He did not approve of the king's marital adventures, and in 1536 broke a long and ominous silence to denounce them in strident terms. Henry VIII's propagandists called him a traitor. He replied that 'Rome is my country'. In response Henry tried to have him assassinated, and judicially murdered most of his family, including his aged mother, for the unpardonable crime of having Pole blood in their veins. Pope Paul III compounded matters by making Pole a cardinal. He became the English government's favourite bogeyman, an icon of treachery.

But Pole's Catholicism was reforming as well as unstinting. In Italy he became intimately involved with the *spirituali*, especially as they found some cautious favour at the papal court. He was fully supportive of one of the great might-have-been projects of the Reformation era: the summit conference at the German city of Regensburg in 1541 between leading Catholic and Protestant theologians which successfully thrashed out an agreed formula for understanding the doctrine of salvation, the issue which had sparked the Protestant schism to begin with. Agonizingly, however, the summit then foundered on the authority of the pope and the nature of the mass. The following year, Pope Paul III made Pole one of three legates who were to preside over the planned General Council of the Catholic Church, which eventually assembled at the northern Italian city of Trento in 1545.

The Council eventually rejected Pole's Lutheran-inflected views of salvation in favour of a more robustly traditional formulation, but Pole and the *spirituali* were not out of the game yet. When Paul III died in 1549, the 49-year-old Pole was the early favourite to succeed him. In one early tally, the conclave came within a single vote of the two-thirds majority which would have elected the second English pope. It is another tantalizing might-have-been: a young, idealistic and energetically reforming pontiff, determined both to hold the centre and also to widen the circle in an effort to bring home as many of the sundered Protestant brethren as possible. In the event, Pole's candidacy failed partly because he himself was reluctant to press his case, and was happy to agree on a compromise candidate; and partly because Cardinal Carafa, one of Pole's former brethren among the *spirituali*, accused him of straying from an innocent wish for reunion into a dalliance with heresy.

This would be merely the tale of one eccentric expatriate's near misses were it not for the second reason to imagine England's Catholic Reformation: the greatest might-have-been of all. For in 1553, England's young, Protestant king Edward VI – whom we will meet properly in later chapters – died, and the inept attempt he had made to rig the succession soon unravelled. The throne fell to his eldest sister, Mary, a committed Catholic whose firm intention from the beginning was to end her native land's 20-year nightmare of schism and heresy and return it to its historic role as a bastion of the Church of Rome. To that end, she and Pope Julius III immediately agreed that the obvious person to negotiate this Catholic restoration, and then to serve as Archbishop of Canterbury, was Reginald Pole.

As it turned out, England's Catholic restoration was short-lived. On 17 November 1558, Queen Mary and Cardinal Pole succumbed to quite different diseases within hours of each other, and the new Queen Elizabeth led the country back into schism. But as historians have dug into this brief episode in recent years, it has become quite clear that the Catholicism of Mary's reign was neither doomed nor a medieval throwback. It was, rather, a taste of what England's

Catholic Reformation might have been. One key to this is that it was a coalition. It brought a few exiled idealists like Pole together with the majority of English churchmen who, like the now aged Bishop Tunstall, had gone reluctantly along with Henry VIII's desires. Those two parties did not entirely trust each other and had subtly different agendas, but – at least for as long as the queen lived – the result was a creative and constructive tension rather than a damaging rivalry.

So the queen restored a few dissolved monasteries, but these refoundations – especially her flagship foundation at Westminster Abbey – were not mere revivals: they were a blueprint for a new, slimmed-down monastic estate that would be at the rest of the nation's service. More importantly, the bishops launched a programme of mass education, bypassing the fact that few clergy were equipped to preach properly by providing them with pre-printed homilies and resource books. Lay initiative was mobilized to rebuild a properly equipped popular Catholicism in the parishes. Pole and his allies, meanwhile, deliberately avoided public polemical combat with their Protestant rivals, on the principle that wrestling in mud taints winners as well as losers.

They chose to deal with those Protestant rivals in another way. The need to enforce the boundaries of orthodoxy had explicitly been part of the Catholic Reformation from the beginning. England's greatest Christian humanist, Thomas More, was also its most pitiless hammer of heretics. As Lord Chancellor, head of the kingdom's secular courts, he worked with rare energy alongside like-minded bishops to arrest suspected heretics and to roll up their networks. He was involved in half a dozen burnings, although there is no hard evidence to support the persistent rumours that he had prisoners tortured. This purge ended when he was forced out of office in 1532, but (as we shall see) trials and executions for heresy would continue apace through Henry VIII's reign, abating only under Edward VI. When Mary restored Catholicism, she also restored the old persecutory apparatus.

The scale of the burnings during her reign – 298 known executions, plus 20 deaths in prison – had no precedent in England and few in Europe, although by modern standards of mass killing it looks positively amateurish. It was, in an important sense, unintended. Mary and her bishops expected that most of those charged with heresy would give way, and recant their beliefs to save their lives, as had usually been the case in the past. The new mettle of these Protestants was a surprise to everyone, including themselves. But when the regime's bluff was called, it chose to follow through. The result was a four-year purge that began with the most prominent bishops and preachers and spread out to entire clandestine Protestant congregations.

It was not simply an English phenomenon. Persecution of Protestantism was simultaneously ramping up in France and the Netherlands. And in 1555, two years into Mary's restoration, Cardinal Pole's old colleague and rival Cardinal Carafa was elected Pope Paul IV. His reformism had now taken a grim turn. Having purged Rome of infidels by creating the city's first ghetto for Jews, he now set out to purge Catholic Christendom of error. In 1559 he would promulgate the first modern index of prohibited books. But before that he renewed his feud with Pole, whom he was now convinced was a crypto-Protestant. Farcically, by 1558 the most serious opponent of Pole's mission to rebuild English Catholicism was the pope, who was refusing to allow any English bishops to be appointed and had begun inquisitorial proceedings against Pole himself.

To modern eyes all this repression looks like a betrayal of the energetic creativity of Catholic reform, just as Thomas More's humane sophistication seems to sit ill with his merciless pursuit of heresy. That was not how it seemed at the time. Drawing ever more Christians into the Church's circle of holiness was one thing; standing by while a handful of heretics tried to pull the whole structure down was another. The deeper your concern for God's people, the more you will want to defend them from wolves. If Carafa's increasingly paranoid suspicions were self-defeating, Mary and Pole's anti-heresy campaign was probably working. The Protestant leaders were either arrested and executed, or forced into exile. The process of breaking up their wider networks of support was well under way. As Carafa had learned when he revived the Inquisition in Italy in 1542, and cracked down on the freewheeling experiments of the *spirituali*, persecution sometimes works.

So, in another world, the legacy of England's Catholic Reformation might have been a walled garden: a flourishing, well-ordered, diverse, creative and firmly managed Catholic England, renewing itself from its own energies, where everyone knew what was and was not permitted to be said and thought, and where, because everyone understood the consequences of straying too far, no one did so. But that is not how things turned out.

For after Mary's death in 1558, she was remembered for her wave of persecution, not for the creativity of her religious rebuilding. The nickname 'Bloody Mary' was coined a century later, when the burnings were still vividly recalled. The lesson was taken to heart: this is what Catholics do when they have the chance. English-speaking Protestants across the world lovingly burnished the memories of those horrors, and used them to justify persecution, discrimination and periodic outbreaks of pre-emptive violence.

The most enduring legacy of England's abortive Catholic Reformation, then, is a prejudice so pervasive that, even in our own supposedly secular times, most non-Catholic English-speaking people scarcely know they harbour it. True, anti-Catholicism is not what it once was. In the seventeenth century, fears of Catholicism helped to make the English Civil War seem a necessary act of self-defence, justified systematic massacres and mass expulsions of Irish Catholics, drove a decade-long political crisis based on the fear of what another Catholic monarch might do, and sparked a grimly farcical panic about an entirely invented 'Popish Plot' in 1678–81 which resulted in at least 22 executions. A century on, an attempt to loosen anti-Catholic laws in 1778–80 led to mass demonstrations, eventually put down by the army with a death toll almost equalling Mary's body count. Further attempts at legal relaxation caused paralysing political crises in 1801 and 1829. The restoration of the Catholic hierarchy in England in 1850 provoked a wave of protest, including a 'Grand Anti-popish Procession' against the 'Papal Aggression'.

In the twentieth and twenty-first centuries, this legacy of prejudice has been at its most explicit in Northern Ireland, where loyalist murals regularly feature the Marian burnings. But it has persisted more quietly elsewhere. British law still requires the monarch to be a Protestant and until 2011 banned a monarch from marrying a Catholic. Britain has not yet had a Catholic prime minister. Tony Blair converted to Catholicism shortly after leaving office in 2007, and his inclination to do so was an open secret well before that, but he plainly felt that to convert while in office would risk stirring up troubles best left to slumber. The United States has only elected one Catholic president, John F. Kennedy: the nimble care with which he had to navigate accusations that he would take orders from Rome, and the refusal of a stubborn minority of American Protestants to countenance voting for a slave of Antichrist, are not as deep in the past as we might like to think. The sexual abuse scandals which have broken over the Catholic Church in the twenty-first century are appalling in their own right, but to understand the way in which the story has gripped the wider culture, while comparable scandals in other religious or secular institutions have not, we need to appreciate how they have fallen into long-established patterns of anti-Catholicism, in societies still primed to hear tales of a cruel hierarchy whose religion is a cloak for its authoritarian instincts and its brutal lusts. Of course, both the Marian persecution and the modern abuse crisis are real. So is a centuries-old, only half-acknowledged fact of life in much of the English-speaking world: anti-Catholicism is the last respectable prejudice.

2

Deformation

In some countries the Protestant Reformation was a mass movement. Protestantism in much of Germany, Switzerland, the Netherlands, Poland, Hungary, Scotland and even France was not exactly 'popular' – everywhere, a great many people loathed the new religion – but it was certainly a movement 'from below', in which nobles, townspeople and sometimes even peasants mobilized to create new religious worlds in the teeth of opposition from their rulers. In a few other territories, the story was reversed. In Sweden, some German territories, Ireland and England, the initiative came from the top. Populations that had shown at best limited interest in religious innovations were suddenly forced to embrace them.

The tale of how England's Protestant Reformation was rammed down its unwilling throat is not the whole truth, but it is a part of the truth which most English people have been too ready to forget – except, that is, for England's persistent Catholic minority, who have made this narrative their own. We apparently owe the most compelling one-word summary of the story to John Proctor, a schoolmaster whose unheroic but sincere path through the dangerous confusion of mid-sixteenth-century England stands for many others' struggles. Proctor was born in 1521, and so was still only a boy when Henry VIII broke with Rome in 1534. From 1537 to 1546 he was a student at Oxford, the more traditionalist of England's two universities, and he persuaded himself that the 'noble Henry, King of Kings' was merely stamping out superstition and abuses. Thereafter he became a schoolmaster in Kent, where he watched the accelerating radicalism of Edward VI's reign with dismay, trying to hold on to a disappearing religious centre ground. Once Mary became queen and Catholicism was restored, a sorrier and wiser Proctor celebrated the end of England's experiment with heresy. The nation had learned the hard way that the Protestants offered 'not . . . faithful religion, but deceitful delusion . . . not truthful preaching, but ruthful [woeful] breaking of all Christian orders; not right reformation of things amiss, but devilish deformation of things that were well'. He could not know that within five years both he and his queen would be dead; and that Catholic England's Deformation had only just begun.

The story of the English Deformation is one of religious change successfully imposed on an unwilling population. To modern sensibilities, reared as we are on the democratic notion that the will of the people ought naturally to prevail, this sounds as if it should have been impossible, but Tudor England was in no sense a democracy. The normal place of its common people was to endure and obey. However, very little about what happened to England's religious life in the sixteenth century was 'normal'. As the time-honoured rules of religious politics were torn up, the people who deplored what was happening sometimes simply acquiesced, but sometimes also held the changes at bay, negotiated with or – in some cases – openly resisted them. Occasionally they even succeeded.

The story begins in the late 1520s, as the people of England became aware that their king was proposing to throw over his long-standing, faithful and pious wife, Queen Catherine, in favour of a scheming, younger, French-educated rival, and to declare his daughter a bastard in the process. This proposal could be defended in terms of canon law or reason of state, but not in common morality. Subjects' opinions about their monarchs' marriages did not usually matter very much, but once it became clear that Henry VIII was planning to throw out the pope, the Vicar of Christ, as well as his lawful wife, popular distaste acquired a harder edge. In 1532 the Warwickshire MP Sir George Throckmorton accused the king to his face of having 'meddled' both with Anne Boleyn's sister and her mother – a double accusation so shocking that the king, caught off balance, effectively conceded the first part in his eagerness to deny the second. The fact that Throckmorton could get away with such insolence shows how fragile politics was becoming. Nor was he speaking only for himself. His warning – or threat – to the king was that if Henry persisted, 'such feuds and intestine divisions would result therefrom as to completely destroy and subvert the whole kingdom'. It was no idle fantasy. England had had dynastic civil wars within living memory.

As Henry's battle with his wife turned into a wider war with the Church, his subjects chose sides. It was all too obvious that many of the king's supporters were self-serving careerists, while most of his opponents were taking their stands on principle and had nothing to gain from doing so. John Fisher, the elderly and pious Bishop of Rochester, was England's most internationally eminent theologian; he became Queen Catherine's earliest and most consistent defender. As the stakes became plainer, other, more politically cautious bishops began to find their nerve too. Stephen Gardiner, the young and ambitious Bishop of Winchester, derailed his own hitherto effortless political ascent in 1532 when he discovered he could no longer collaborate with his king's schemes. Even Archbishop William Warham of Canterbury, a long-serving and generally pliable prelate, was finding it impossible to ignore his conscience. Fisher and Warham were both connected to a perhaps more dangerous figure: Elizabeth Barton, the 'Holy Maid of Kent', a servant girl turned nun whose pious visions were acquiring a dangerously political edge. She claimed God had told her that if the king remarried he would forfeit his throne and be deposed within a month. For a brief moment, she looked like a new Joan of Arc, the peasant girl who a century before had helped to drive another English king from one of his thrones.

That these threats never came to a head was chiefly due to the man who, at that disastrous royal audience with Throckmorton, intervened to limit the damage: Thomas Cromwell. He sidelined the conscience-stricken bishops, paralysed by their twin loyalties to God's Church and to his anointed king. Warham had the decency to die in August 1532, just in time to be replaced at Canterbury by a rapidly promoted scholar, Thomas Cranmer, chosen for only one reason: he genuinely supported the king's twin grievances with his wife and with the pope. Gardiner and others were frozen out of favour until, one by one, they gave in and reconciled themselves to the new world. Only two prominent naysayers refused to buckle: Fisher and his friend Thomas More. The pope tried to save Fisher by making him a cardinal, which enraged rather than deterred the king. More tried to save himself by shrewd legal tactics, which only compelled Cromwell to concoct evidence against him. By the time both men were beheaded in the summer of 1535, they were almost alone.

The threat of popular resistance had already been seen off, at least temporarily. Elizabeth Barton shared Joan of Arc's fate: she and her supporters were rounded up in late 1533, and she was forced publicly to denounce her own prophecies as fake before being judicially murdered. In the meantime, Cromwell developed an unprecedented and, in its quiet way, revolutionary policy. Every adult male in England was required by law to swear an oath recognizing the king's marriage to Anne Boleyn and also, by implication, his newly claimed 'supremacy' over the English Church. To refuse to swear was to invite a treason charge. The fact that virtually the entire nation complied demonstrates the regime's strength. The fact that the regime needed to extort such an oath demonstrates its weakness. Kings do not normally need their subjects' consent to marry. By requiring the entire population to express an opinion on the subject, it opened up undreamed-of possibilities for political participation. It was the first time the English (male) population as a whole had ever been formally drawn into politics.

It was also a sign that Henry VIII's Reformation – as it was not yet called – would be more than a matter for lawyers and bishops. Already it was reaching into the parishes. Orders went out to ban the prayers said for the pope at every mass, and to ensure that preachers extolled the king's newly claimed title. As yet these were clouds no bigger than a man's hand, and most parishes accommodated them with no more than a few hand-inked corrections to their liturgical books. But they were harbingers. Cromwell was soon made the king's Vice-gerent in Spirituals – empowering him, a mere layman, to exercise the Royal Supremacy over the Church on his master's behalf – and quickly redoubled the reforming efforts he had once made for Cardinal Wolsey. Ominous initiatives arrived one by one. Commissioners travelled the country reporting on the property and income of every parish and searching, with undisguised malice, for reports of moral lapses in monastic houses. A royal progress to the west of England in 1535 helped to cool anxieties there: Henry VIII was always superb at the theatrics of monarchy. The north, meanwhile, simmered. In the spring of 1536, the new queen to whose legitimacy the nation had just sworn was suddenly declared an adulterous, incestuous traitor, the marriage was invalidated and she was beheaded. What were the people to think? Rumours flew. A new set of royal injunctions ordered that every church keep a comprehensive register of all baptisms, marriages and funerals. Did that mean that all these services were now going to be taxed? How far could the king and his clique of heretics and opportunists push their luck?

The last straw, as it turned out, was an amped-up Wolsey-era policy: putting monasteries to better use. Wolsey had seized carefully selected houses for carefully pious purposes, but in his last year in power, he had secured new powers to repurpose monastic property on a larger scale. These powers lapsed with his fall, but Parliament considered several such schemes during the early 1530s. Finally, in the spring of 1536, Cromwell secured a blunt but effective piece of legislation. All religious houses with an annual income of less than £200 would be 'dissolved'; that is, closed down, with the monks and nuns either released from their vows or transferred to other houses, and the monasteries' lands and goods being placed in the care of the Church's Supreme Head, Henry VIII. The pretence that this was about reform, not plunder, was scarcely maintained.

The commissioners setting out to enforce the policy in the autumn of 1536 touched a match to an already tinder-dry bonfire of popular grievance – especially in the north, where parish churches were thinly scattered, and monasteries and their services were integral to many lay Christians' lives. The revolts began in Lincolnshire and rapidly spread north. The largest and most dangerous rising, centred in Yorkshire, called itself the 'Pilgrimage of Grace for the Commonwealth'. These 'Pilgrims' marched under a banner of Christ's wounds and, ominously following the example the regime had set them, bound themselves with a common oath. They declared their loyalty to their king, but were also 'gnawn in their conscience with spreading heresies, suppression of houses of religion and other matters touching the commons' wealth'. They demanded not only that the monasteries be left alone, but that the heretics around the king should be purged, the bastardized Princess Mary restored to the line of succession and, not least, that the pope's authority should be acknowledged again. Within weeks there were forty thousand rebels in arms in the north, and alarming rumours of sympathizers in the south too. The furious king scrambled together what forces he could, but it quickly became clear that, if it came to a fight, he and his Reformation could not win.

It was the moment when popular will could, conceivably, have stopped the English Reformation, and it did not happen. The king did not win a battle, but he did not need to. He outlasted and outmanoeuvred his opponents, lulled them into dispersing with empty promises, found pretexts to abandon those promises as soon as it was safe to do so, rounded up and slaughtered the ringleaders, and imposed martial law on the north. It was a turning-point, but not the one the Pilgrims had sought. For now that the king's opponents had showed their hand and lost, who was going to stand in his way?

Cromwell, whose life had hung by a thread while the Pilgrims' army was on the march, now redoubled his efforts, and the Reformation reached into parish life like never before. In 1538 a systematic assault was made on shrines, relics and sites of pilgrimage across the country, with once-venerated objects being publicly ridiculed and then privately melted down, burned or pulverized. A swathe of traditional saints' days and fasting days were banned. Cowed, disorientated and concerned to save what fragments of their communities' former property they could, most parishes mutely complied. And by 1540, Cromwell had dissolved not only the smaller monasteries targeted in 1536, but every single religious house in England: the biggest transfer of landed wealth in English history.

It was in 1540, however, that Cromwell's luck finally ran out, when a sudden, capricious surge of the king's rage cost him his head. Combined with a law passed the previous year, the so-called Act of Six Articles, which declared that the king would hold fast to a series of traditional Catholic doctrines, Cromwell's fall raised hopes that the worst was over. But Henry VIII had come to enjoy his self-image as the purifier of the English Church, along with the accompanying profits. A long-delayed royal progress to the north of England in 1541 brought a shocked king face to face with the continued veneration of images and statues there, and a fresh purge of 'idolatry' followed. Archbishop Cranmer persuaded the king to introduce a new English-language form for processional prayers in 1544. Those prayers did not bring victory in the ruinously expensive wars with

France and Scotland, and so in late 1545 a new law gave the king the power to seize the endowments of chantries, colleges and virtually any other church foundation he pleased. In 1546 he seriously considered systematically stripping the assets of England's two universities, before deciding that it tickled his fancy more to found an ostentatious new college at each of them instead.

By then Henry was already seriously ill. When he finally died in early 1547, his crown passed to his nine-year-old son. The question was, who would rule in the boy's name? And whether by chance or not, in the last two months of the old king's life, the murderous dance of court politics had lurched decisively against religious conservatives. When the music stopped on 27 January, Bishop Gardiner, the leading conservative churchman, was once again frozen out of favour, and the Duke of Norfolk, the leading conservative nobleman, was only hours from being beheaded. (The king's death saved him: the new regime was a little less homicidal.) In what amounted to an internal coup, the government of England was seized by a determined clique of Protestants, headed by the king's swashbuckling uncle, Edward Seymour, the brother of Henry VIII's third wife. Seymour became Duke of Somerset and Lord Protector. England has never been ruled by a government whose views are so sharply out of step with the country as a whole.

There was more to the programme which this government pushed insistently through over the next six years than simple destruction. Yet traditionalists could be forgiven if that was all they saw. A new set of royal injunctions ordered every parish to 'take away, utterly extinct, and destroy all shrines, covering of shrines, all . . . pictures, paintings, and all other monuments of feigned miracles, pilgrimages, idolatry and superstition: so that there remain no memory of the same'. Even before the injunctions were issued, it had begun. Protestant provocateurs were attacking images, rightly confident that no one would stop them. In November 1547, even the great 'rood' (crucifix) in St Paul's Cathedral in London was desecrated. Printers began producing outspokenly evangelical works, viciously mocking pieties that had once been universally respected. No one was willing to print books that made the opposite case. In case parish priests were inclined to argue, the regime suspended all preaching licences until a new wave of preachers could be approved. In the meantime, an official set of printed sermons was sent to every parish, and reluctant priests were required to read them aloud.

The regime's determination was sharpened by its desperate need for cash, as Somerset hurled himself into a fresh and ultimately doomed war with Scotland and France. In late 1547 the regime did what Henry VIII had threatened, and dissolved all chantries and collegiate churches, the universities alone excepted. This second dissolution is now less well known than the assault on the monasteries, but its impact was comparable. Another swathe of property passed into royal hands. These endowments had supported many thousands of priests, almost as many as held parish posts, allowing them to act as teachers, scriveners or in other roles vital to local communities; they were now pensioned off on a pittance. The prayers they had said and the sacraments they had celebrated on behalf of the deceased parents, grandparents and children of their parishes now simply lapsed. The principal link between the worlds of the living and the dead had been severed.

The ratchet of change accelerated. In 1548, as the chant-ries and colleges were being shuttered, traditional liturgical practices like the use of holy water were banned and a new English-language order for the mass was implemented. One by one, the senior clergy who objected were deprived of office, imprisoned or driven into exile; but not killed, a sign that this regime lacked both Henry VIII's self-assurance and his vengefulness. In 1549, the most imposing physical monuments of the old religion – the roods and the consecrated stone altars that could be found in every parish church – were destroyed. Not a single medieval English rood now survives. An ominously titled Act of Uniformity required that, from the feast of Pentecost, every parish abandon its old liturgy in favour of a complete new English order of service, the Book of Common Prayer.

Again, we might imagine that there is only so much unwelcome radicalism that rulers can foist on their people before they push back. In the summer of 1549, a wave of unrest swept across much of England, stirred chiefly by economic woes. The population had been growing for decades, slowly pushing up rents, impoverishing peasants and enriching landowners. That situation was now sharply worsened by a surge of inflation, as a cash-strapped govern-ment began debasing the coinage to fund its wars. There was rioting and looting, and landowners were attacked. There were encampments, as alarmingly well-ordered troops of protesters assembled to petition their rulers for redress. Some of them wrapped themselves in the old religion. In Hampshire and Sussex there was talk of marching under a banner of Christ's wounds, like the Pilgrims of 1536.

In the south-west, England's most persistently rebellious corner, it went beyond encampments. There had been disturbances in Cornwall in 1547 and 1548, including the lynching of a senior cleric. The rebellion of 1549 was much more serious. The Cornish rebels focused not on economic woes, but on religious change. In 1536 the trigger had been the assault on the monasteries. This time it was the new Prayer Book, which the rebels dismissed as a 'Christmas game', a parody of true religion. They marched east, hoping to rally the region to their cause.

But they made it no farther than Devon, and the support they found even there was less than they had hoped. The city of Exeter held out against them, before being relieved by a royal army. The rebels were now pursued west, cornered and slaughtered, despite attempts to surrender. Dozens of priests, the presumed firestarters of the rebellion, were killed in reprisals. Once again, a moment when the popular will might have forced a change of direction had come and gone.

For across England, most of the 'campers' seem if anything to have aligned themselves with the new religion, not the old. Somerset's favoured preachers had spent two years blaming the country's woes on the greed of landowners and presenting their own moral crusade as the solution – a stance which may seem naïve but was, it must be said, sincerely meant. Whether the 'campers' of 1549 truly accepted such a claim or merely reckoned it was prudent to adopt their rulers' cant, a great many of them couched their economic complaints in the regime's religious rhetoric. Somerset, in truth unable to do anything else, pretended to listen to them. Most of them dispersed without serious incident as the summer wore on. Only in Norfolk did a combination of specific local woes and a ham-handed government response lead to serious violence, which ended with a mercenary army slaughtering thousands at the battle of Dussindale on 27 August 1549.

The political fallout from this summer of chaos was dramatic. Somerset was forced out of power, and the government took on a steely new face. Its dominant figure was now the victor of Dussindale, the earl of Warwick (soon to be made Duke of Northumberland). But once the dust cleared from an autumn of furious political intrigue, it was clear that this reconstituted regime was not going to change its religious policy. It was still dominated by convinced Protestants, including the precocious young king himself. The ratchet of change accelerated again: further asset-stripping, extending even to parishes' communion silver; a new, more radical revision of the Prayer Book; a new set of Forty-Two Articles of Religion, defining the English Church as unambiguously Reformed Protestant. Once again, a dangerous brush with popular opposition did not weaken the reformers, but strengthened them.

The political potency of religious traditionalism in England was at its lowest ever ebb during the final three and a half years of Edward VI's reign. The remaining conservative churchmen were prised out of office and replaced with Protestant zealots. Their lay supporters were left mute and bewildered, many of them clinging to the fantasy that when the king grew up he would be their good lord and restore true religion. These people had gone along with Henry VIII's Reformation, swearing to accept him as Supreme Head of the Church and trusting that he and his heirs would be true to the faith they hoped he shared with them. Now that trust was going septic, but what could they do, apart from utter helpless prayers?

And then, in the summer of 1553, those prayers were answered. Instead of growing up to be a Protestant tyrant, the 15-year-old king died of tuberculosis. He tried to fix the succession in favour of a young Protestant cousin, who just so happened to be married to the Duke of Northumberland's son, but the plan was carried out too ineptly and smelled too much of trickery to succeed. Instead, in the century's most successful rebellion, Henry VIII's cast-off eldest daughter, Mary, swept to the throne. The wave of popular support that she rode to power reflected her perceived legitimacy more than her religion as such, but it was immediately obvious that England's 20-year heretical nightmare was over. The people who had been cowed into collaboration by Henry VIII and bewildered into silence by Edward VI could now cheer. Perhaps they were not actively demanding the full-scale return to papal obedience that followed, but they certainly accepted it. That at least we can deduce from the effort and expense they devoted to restoring their looted parish churches over the next five years, in the midst of continuing economic woes and, latterly, two devastating years of epidemics and near-famine.

Of course, their relief was short-lived. Although Queen Mary quickly married, the royal pregnancy which was announced and widely celebrated turned out to be a mirage. When she died in 1558, she was as childless as her young brother had been. Unlike him, she was too wise or too cowardly to try to rig the succession, and accepted that the throne would pass to her Protestant half-sister Elizabeth. The survivors of Edward VI's Protestant establishment reassembled. It looked as if it was all going to begin again, and as if nothing had changed.

That is not quite how things turned out. True, after a few months of delicate politicking, the new queen enacted a set of religious policies which broadly reset the dial to where it had been in the last year of King Edward's life. There was once again a Prayer Book enforced by an Act of Uniformity and a sweeping set of royal injunctions banning all the pieties and ornaments so painstakingly restored under Mary. There was almost a clean sweep of the bishops, many of Elizabeth's newcomers being radicals who had returned from drinking at the wellsprings of Protestant purity in Switzerland and Germany. The restored monasteries were closed, and royal commissioners patiently went from church to church purging them of 'idolatry'. The most obvious difference was that, this time, death did not intervene. Elizabeth kept her so-called settlement of religion in place for almost 45 years, and her successor James I did no more than tweak it. England's religion was not only forced into a new shape, but held there long enough that the plaster set.

But this bleak story of England's Deformation is not quite adequate. For one thing, as we shall see, by the start of Elizabeth's reign it was becoming impossible to ignore the fact that England genuinely did have a mass Protestant movement, albeit still a small one. For another, Elizabeth's Reformation was less a simple restoration of her brother's than a kind of effigy of it, without its relentless drive to uproot. Her own idiosyncratic but stubborn affection for the old ways made its mark, and helped some of her traditionalist subjects to feel that they were not entirely friendless in this new world.

Most importantly, for those traditionalists, the world had been transformed by Mary's reign. She had failed to save Catholic England, but she had saved English Catholicism. The traditionalists who had been paralysed and impotent under Edward VI were, under their new heretical monarch, energized and grimly ready. Elizabeth hoped to persuade a number of Mary's bishops to accept her new settlement: men like Cuthbert Tunstall who had openly supported Henry VIII's Reformation and had tried to work with Edward VI's. All but one of them refused. The battle lines were now clear: English Catholics – a term we can now begin to use with meaning – knew where they stood. They had lost their taste for helpless conformity.

Most of the stubborn Marian ex-bishops lived out their lives in Elizabeth's prisons. A younger generation of leaders chose exile, plotting their eventual return. They bombarded the new regime with printed polemics and worked to drum up Continent-wide support for their cause, the most obvious fruit of which was a new seminary for English Catholics, established at Douai in the Netherlands in 1568.

But most of those who were now thinking of themselves as Catholics remained in England. Some chose to be 'recusants', defiantly refusing to attend Protestant worship and paying fines as a result; others became 'church papists', cloaking their Catholic allegiance in a show of outward conformity. What no one knew was how strong these Catholic remnants were. For a decade, Elizabeth and her ministers sedulously avoided confronting or provoking them, restricting themselves to carefully implementing the new settlement, progressively easing Catholics out of positions of influence, slowly placing a new generation of clerics in the parishes. The regime hoped that time was on their side; and feared that if 1536 or 1549 were repeated, they might not be lucky a third time.

The phoney war was brought to an end when a political crisis that had been simmering since the beginning of the reign boiled over. The crisis was the succession. Queen Elizabeth was unmarried and childless, and most of the serious candidates to succeed her were Catholics. This made her Reformation feel much less secure at the time than it looks in retrospect. By far the most plausible of those Catholic candidates was her cousin Mary, the queen of Scots, who spent the 1560s trying to position herself as Elizabeth's successor. The effort was so spectacularly unsuccessful that in 1567 Mary was deposed from her Scottish throne and by 1568 was imprisoned in England, suspected of having murdered her second husband. But as long as she breathed, she remained Elizabeth's likeliest heir. For Catholics, the prospect of a new queen who could reverse their fortunes at a stroke was too much to resist. In the autumn of 1569, amid a ferment of schemes and plots, two Catholic earls in England's north-east stumbled into rebellion. Soon most of the region was in arms. There were bonfires of Protestant Prayer Books. The Catholic mass was celebrated in Durham Cathedral. The earls prepared to march south.

And once again, the threat evaporated. Too few men rallied to the earls' banner. Their hopes hinged on liberating the imprisoned Scottish queen, but she was whisked south long before they could reach her. A royal army was assembled with daunting speed, but met no resistance. The earls' small force ebbed away as they ran out of money, and they fled to Scotland. England's Catholics evidently had spirit, but, it was suddenly plain, they no longer had numbers. A second, desperate rising in Cumberland was bloodily put down in February 1570, and Elizabeth's soldiers now took full advantage of their opponents' evident weakness. What followed was a systematic, punitive campaign of repression without precedent in Tudor England. Suspects were tortured. Explicit quotas of 20 to 40 per cent were set for the proportion of suspects who should be executed. At least six hundred were killed. There was little pretence of justice: this was exemplary terror, and it worked. Catholic England would never rebel again.

The survivors, both at home and abroad, faced two choices. The first was laid out for them by Pope Pius V, who, in the wake of the risings, issued a bull excommunicating England's heretical queen and calling on her subjects to rise up against her. In this defiant spirit, the seminary at Douai and the others that joined it were training English Catholic exiles and sending them back home as missionaries, stiffening spines, keeping underground networks alive and bringing the cutting edge of Counter-Reformation Catholicism to England's shires. In 1579, a recently founded English college in Rome itself was taken over by the age's most formidable missionary order, the Jesuits, who quickly made themselves the leaders of English Catholic resistance. This movement's message to ordinary Catholics was to be resolute, to shun conformity and to wait and pray. Meanwhile, the high command laid plans. Elizabeth might be assassinated. The Scottish queen might be freed. The king of Spain's Armada might transport a Catholic army to Kent, and an army of English Catholics might rise up to join him.

These hopes were not ridiculous. The regime took them immensely seriously. But realistic or not, the one thing we know is that they came to nothing. At best, they helped England's Catholics to become a stubborn minority, cherishing their martyrs and holding to the faith of their fathers for centuries to come. The cost was high. It was already plain that the Elizabethan state was perfectly ready to shed Catholic blood. The seminary priests met a storm of persecution. Henry VIII had executed dozens of papal loyalists for treason, but no one had died in this way between 1544 and 1573. A trickle of deaths in the 1570s turned into a flood in the 1580s and 1590s: nearly two hundred in all. The fines for recusancy were ramped up to unpayable levels. Torture was again authorized. Simply to be a Catholic became, in effect, presumptive evidence of treason.

So it is no surprise that some English Catholics were tempted by the other choice: to emphasize their loyalty to their queen, and to try to find a way to practise their faith without betraying their country. The Jesuits staunchly opposed such compromises, and by the late 1590s the English mission was bitterly divided, with the regime deliberately stirring up trouble among the opposing Catholic parties as best it could. Rome eventually had to intervene to settle the dispute, and the compromisers were slapped down. As if to emphasize the point, in 1605 one group of very uncompromising Catholics nearly pulled off the most audacious plot of them all: to blow up the new King James I and his entire Parliament with gunpowder.

Yet it was the compromisers who had time on their side. There would be no more spectacular plots. Regular persecution came to an end too. King James's diplomatic opening to Europe's Catholic powers, and especially his son King Charles I's marriage to a Catholic princess who was allowed to practise her faith at court, gave English Catholics friends in high places once again. There were spasms of bloody panic during the Civil War of the 1640s, and the Exclusion Crisis and the imaginary 'Popish Plot' of the late 1670s, but aside from such feverishly paranoid moments, it slowly became clear that a kind of equilibrium had been reached. England's Deformation was not going to be reversed by some political *deus ex machina*. Nor were

England's Catholics going to be exterminated. They and their Protestant neighbours would have to work out a way of living together.

The Sussex town of Arundel points the way. This was the realm of the Fitzalan earls of Arundel, who were staunchly loyal both to their Catholic religion and to their Protestant monarchs. Once upon a time, the town's collegiate church had also housed the Fitzalan family's chapel, with a simple iron gate separating the two. When Henry VIII seized the church's assets in 1544, the earl secured a coup: he managed to buy back the chapel as his private property. And so from then until now, St Nicholas, Arundel has been an entity at once singular and a microcosm of all England: a divided church housing a frozen conflict. Most of the building is the Protestant (or now, rather, Anglican) parish church, where the monarch is acknowledged as Supreme Governor. But on the other side of the gate – a gate that still stands, that was never unlocked between 1544 and 1977, and has only been opened a handful of times since – stands a Catholic chapel. This was of course illegal, but as long as the Fitzalans and their heirs the Howards pretended to conceal it, successive Protestant governments were willing to play along.

The pretence that England was no longer a Catholic country was simply the same game played on a grander scale. In fact, Catholicism is built into the very architecture of post-Reformation England. To ignore the fact that only a gate separates the two takes a continuous effort of the will. Whether you see that gate as a disfiguring scar, or as the kind of fence that makes for good neighbours, is a matter of taste. But nothing would be simpler, or more destabilizing, than to swing it open.

3

Tudor Reformation

'The Reformation', conventionally, means the process by which parts of Catholic Europe became Protestant. That process happened in England, but we should not be too distracted by it. From the point of view of law and of the sinews of the English state, the doctrinal, devotional and cultural transformations were so much froth: a by-product, or even a useful distraction. The English Reformation was a political event more than a religious one. It brought the English state, in the sense we now know it, into being; and it fixed the relationships between the nations of Britain and Ireland that we still enjoy or endure today.

Medieval politics was marked by a long dance between 'church' and 'state' – or better, between the 'spiritual' power wielded by the pope, bishops and great abbots, and the 'temporal' power wielded by princes, noblemen and cities. Sometimes these two spheres of power collided spectacularly; sometimes one of them fell into crisis, and the other took the chance to press its advantage; but in general they worked together, recognizing that this was in everyone's interest. Instead of rivals, the spiritual and temporal powers were generally collaborators: staffed by members of the same great families, sharing the same ambitions for godly good order. The temporal powers were the Church's indispensable guardians and patrons. The spiritual power was the monarchs' indispensable reservoir of legitimacy and of bureaucratic expertise.

If pressed, both sides could be persuaded to make dramatic claims. The popes had, since the eleventh century and certainly since the fourteenth, claimed that it was 'absolutely necessary for salvation that every human creature be subject to the Roman Pontiff'; and that this allowed them, if necessary, unilaterally to eject kings from their thrones. Periodically kings pushed back against these claims, whether by defying individual popes or promulgating laws which contradicted papal privileges. In England, most famously, since 1353 the statute of *praemunire* had criminalized attempts by English subjects to appeal to Rome over their king's head.

Beneath this posturing, however, the papacy's political and legal power was ebbing away. It had never truly recovered from the catastrophic schism of 1378–1417, when Europe had been split between two, and eventually three, rival popes. By the early sixteenth century, there was a tacit understanding that the papacy would continue to claim outlandish powers; that monarchs would acknowledge them in theory; and that no pope would risk the embarrassment of trying to exercise them. The papacy's real powers were of a more prosaic kind. Rome's bureaucratic and legal reach was pervasive. The church courts were parallel to, independent of and largely separate from the secular courts of the temporal powers. All Christian rulers had to take into account a body of international law that was beyond their control.

This pattern suited England's first two Tudor kings very well. Like many of their predecessors, Henry VII and Henry VIII loudly proclaimed their loyalty to Rome, quietly defended their own sovereignty, and steadily chipped away at the legal privileges of the English Church. The most controversial issue was whether English churchmen should be subject to the normal criminal law, rather than, as had traditionally been the case, to the rather more lenient church courts. Both kings pared away the Church's privileges. In 1514–15 the leading bishops pushed back against such infringements on their rights. It was a very traditional spat: what is revealing is how it was resolved. The English Church's rapidly rising star, Thomas Wolsey, brokered a deal whereby the king and his secular lawyers conceded the Church's theoretical independence, and the pope then granted the English state legal powers which amounted to those they had been trying to seize. The fiction of spiritual authority was preserved. Real power shifted another notch.

The same pattern held good across much of Europe when the Reformation crisis hit. By the mid-1520s, Martin Luther's movement was offering European princes something unprecedented: a real choice whether or not to remain loyal to Rome. Even those who were never tempted by heresy and schism were aware that the mere fact of choosing gave them a new leverage in dealings with the Church. A canny ruler like King James V of Scots, Henry VIII's nephew, could turn his avowed determination 'to banish the foul Lutheran sect' into a protection racket. King James's loyalty to Rome was real, but its price was swingeing new taxes on the Scottish Church, and lucrative church offices for his own illegitimate infant children. This is how England ought to have gone: banging the drum relentlessly for papal authority while quietly hollowing that authority out.

But in 1527, Henry VIII butted up against one of the papacy's few undisputed powers: matrimonial law. The root of the crisis, plainly, was Henry's determination to trade in his first wife for a newer model, and to do so in good conscience. Yet the tangled specifics of the case made it horribly difficult in law. Henry's queen Catherine of Aragon had, for a few months, been married to his elder brother Prince Arthur, who died in 1502 at the age of 15. She was then pledged to the young Henry, but to marry a brother's widow in this way was normally illegal, and so a dispensation was required from Pope Julius II. The marriage had duly proceeded in 1509, but this unusual situation left a genuine seed of doubt about its legitimacy. Suddenly, in 1527, making that seed sprout into serious grounds for cancelling the marriage became the most urgent political project in England.

Cardinal Wolsey did his best to perform the traditional two-step, protecting the papacy's dignity while securing the outcome his king needed. It was not impossible. The king's legal case was less flimsy than is sometimes supposed; Wolsey was a redoubtable operator; and if all other things had been equal, any pope would have tried to give an English king what he wanted. But the politics were poisonous. Queen Catherine's uncle and defender, the Emperor Charles V, was most reluctant to see England's king marry a woman he saw as a French agent. Since he had actually occupied Rome and briefly imprisoned the pope in 1527, he naturally had a better grasp on the papal attention than the faraway English king. Worse, Henry VIII was every lawyer's nightmare: the client who thinks he knows best. As often as Wolsey tried to soothe papal sensibilities, the king issued a shrill denunciation asserting that neither Julius II nor any other pope had the power to issue such dispensations, or accused Wolsey and other English clergy who were following proper legal procedure of owing more loyalty to a foreign bishop than to their divinely ordained king.

Henry's lustful determination was unshakable; so was his conviction that he was acting in good conscience. Yet he could not browbeat Rome into conceding. Under this intolerable pressure, something had to give, and that something was the king's religious convictions. It is the only moment in this chapter's story when a genuine religious conversion played a decisive role. At some point in 1529 or early 1530, aided by proto-Protestants who had his ear, Henry VIII came to an astonishing conclusion: that Julius II's illegitimate dispensation and his successors' intransigence proved that the papacy as such was entirely without legitimacy. Indeed, it did not even exist. The so-called 'pope' – the word would soon become unsayable – was merely an Italian bishop, heir to lies and conspiracies which deceived Christendom for centuries until he, Henry Tudor, had finally seen through them. Plainly, self-evidently, the Church in England ought to be under the authority of the man God had appointed to rule the country as a whole.

The clergy now seemed to the king to be traitors, kowtowing to a foreign priest and his corrupt laws rather than obeying their lawful sovereign. Henry's first move would have been farcical had anyone dared laugh. He had worked hard to secure Cardinal Wolsey the powers of a papal legate, and to secure him a commission to try the royal marriage case in England. Now, in October 1529, on the basis of those very powers, Wolsey was accused of *praemunire.* The same charge was brought against a group of other senior clerics in 1530, and then in 1531 against the entire body of the English clergy. The Church bought its way out of those immediate charges, but this had never been about money. When the matter came to a head in 1532, the crux was the English Church's independence from royal control. When they demurred at his demands, he accused them of being 'but half our subjects, yea, and scarce our subjects'. Why would bishops even swear an oath to the pope if they were not traitors at heart?

And so, under excruciating pressure, they gave in. The 1532 'Submission of the Clergy', which accepted that Parliament would have ultimate authority over the English Church, was a revolutionary moment: as Thomas More recognized, for he immediately resigned as Lord Chancellor. It reflected the king's furious determination, but also the ruthless strategic brilliance of his new omnicompetent fixer, Thomas Cromwell. With his water-diviner's nose for the subterranean currents of real power, Cromwell had discovered a fount of law that could wash away anything the king wanted to be cleansed. The doctrine that statute law, law enacted by Parliament and approved by the king, was sovereign – absolute, final and beyond question or appeal – has since 1532 become such a truism of the English constitution that it is hard for us to feel the novelty and power of its radical simplicity. It became the procedural trump card wielded by every Tudor regime. As long as a parliament could be persuaded or browbeaten into cooperating (and that was not always the case), a monarch could in law do almost anything.

Cromwell was a pragmatic politician, not a visionary constitutional reformer, but he certainly had a sense of what this new tool he had fashioned could do, and he set about using it. A series of statutes progressively cut the legal ties connecting England to Rome. By the time the 1534 Act of Supremacy formally recognized the king as the Supreme Head, immediately under Christ, of the Church of England, it was almost a fait accompli. Over the years that followed, the scope of statute law was progressively expanded. The principality of Wales, for example, had for centuries been governed on simple royal authority, direct or delegated:

statutes in 1536 and 1543 created a new framework for its government, bringing it into line with English norms. Defining the Church's doctrines, and pursuing those who defied it for heresy, had once been ecclesiastical matters: a series of statutes, especially in 1539 and 1543, secularized them. Witchcraft had been a crime for the church courts – until the Witchcraft Act of 1542. Even the succession to the Crown itself, the untouchable mystery at the heart of a hereditary monarchy, was determined by an Act of 1543. That Act gave no rationale for its peculiar provisions, but it did not need to. Asserting the king-in-parliament's sovereign will was enough.

The most important feature of the 1534 Act of Supremacy was its vagueness. It never explained precisely what the king's new title, 'Supreme Head of the Church', might mean. To define his authority would either be to enrage him by imposing limits on it, to appal Christendom by openly conceding its extent, or both. As a result, the Supremacy was in practice negotiated over the following years and decades, a process which is still continuing. Henry's own view of the Supremacy was dizzyingly high. He saw the sacred kings of ancient Israel as his models, and even toyed with the idea that kingship gave him quasi-priestly authority, such as the power to ordain. He certainly believed he had the authority to micromanage his church's rites, liturgy and doctrines. He publicly argued points of detail with his bishops, and even tried to rewrite one of the Ten Commandments: this most covetous of kings reckoned that God's command not to covet ought only to apply to coveting 'wrongfully or unjustly'. As with several of his other more eye-popping positions, Archbishop Cranmer gently persuaded him to back down on this one, and none of his successors were quite so cavalier. Elizabeth I, recognizing the widespread disquiet with the title of Supreme Head, especially as applied to a woman, chose in 1559 to change it to Supreme Governor – which, since it was still undefined, changed nothing at all in law, but signalled that she intended a certain restraint. Even so, like her father and brother, she launched her religious policy with a sweeping set of royal injunctions for every parish, resting on her sole authority. She also retained a tendency to 'pronounce . . . resolutely and peremptorily' on church matters, as if she were pope – or so her second Archbishop of Canterbury told her. The remark earned him six years' house arrest.

The decisive influence of individual kings' and queens' idiosyncrasies on the post-Reformation Church of England is familiar, but it ought to be more astonishing than it is. Many of the historic oddities of the Church of England – its weird mixture of firmly Protestant doctrinal articles with much more traditional liturgy and ceremonial; its retention of cathedrals, entities which served no coherent purpose in a Protestant church but which nurtured the musical traditions Elizabeth I enjoyed – are the result not of some genius of Anglicanism, but of placing a church under the control of a series of lay people with amateur theological interests and no one to stop them. Alongside these harmless quirks is, naturally, a pervasive commitment to royal authority itself. The Church of England retained bishops, not because they were essential to true Christianity, but because they were appointed by the Crown and served the royal dignity. James I's tart reply to proposals to abolish bishops – 'no bishop, no king' – was about power politics, not theology. Likewise, the ambition cherished by Protestant reformers from Archbishop Cranmer onwards for the English Church to create a fully comprehensive system of moral discipline was repeatedly rebuffed: not for any reason of theological or legal principle, but because no monarch was willing to countenance a new system of church law that might defy secular authority.

Nor was it only a matter of structures and laws. The Church of England's liturgies and its officially authorized homilies – collectively, the most effective broadcast network open to any government in this period – routinely prayed and gave thanks for the monarch, while never so much as hinting that the ruling powers might be anything other than simply righteous. The anniversary of Elizabeth's accession became a feast day marked by a special service of thanksgiving. Every post-Reformation parish church was required to display the royal arms prominently, almost the only pictorial image in these stripped-bare buildings. The Church of England generally refused to recognize 'saints' in the Catholic sense – but with one exception: after 1649, the beheaded Charles I was honoured as the 'Blessed King', 'Charles the Martyr'. In 1662 a commemoration of him was added to the Prayer Book's calendar. Astonishingly, even churches were dedicated to him as a saint; a handful remain to the present. Charles I is not in fact a very credible martyr for Anglicanism – this was the man who had been willing to accept Presbyterianism in 1648, in return for the chance to launch a second, doomed round of civil war. He was, however, certainly a martyr for the Royal Supremacy.

He was also its victim. His father James I had, in his other life as King James VI of Scots, seen up close what happened when a Protestant Reformation wriggled free of royal control, and once he had inherited England's more house-trained Reformation he was determined to maintain its discipline. He succeeded, but had he not done so, his son Charles I's captivation by a particular strand of ceremonial religion might have remained a personal quirk, instead of driving Scotland and much of England to rebel against him in order to preserve their understanding of what a true Reformation was. In turn, his son King James II was driven from his throne in 1688 because England could not tolerate a Catholic as Supreme Governor of the Church. The Royal Supremacy concentrated enormous power in the monarch's hands. As a result, the country eventually decided that the monarch alone could not be trusted to exercise it. Neither Charles I nor James II would have lost their thrones had they not also been Supreme Governor of the Church of England.

For Henry VIII's decision not to define the Royal Supremacy had left open a momentous question: to what extent was the Royal Supremacy vested personally in the monarch, accountable only to God, and to what extent in the monarch-in-parliament, the entity which could create statute law? On the face of it, the 1534 Act of Supremacy was plain: it did not *make* the king Supreme Head of the Church, it merely recognized that God had made him so. Still, it was an Act of Parliament, and the repeated recourse to statute law did make it look very much as if that was where final religious authority lay. The Book of Common Prayer derived its authority from Parliament; so too did the Thirty-Nine Articles of Religion enacted under Elizabeth. Parliament, however, was an increasingly secular body. Without the abbots of the great monasteries seated alongside the bishops, the Lords Spiritual no longer formed a majority in the House of Lords. It seemed a little incongruous that this assembly should wield such spiritual authority. The case for it was made most forcefully by the Elizabethan Church's most enduring theorist, Richard Hooker, who held a very high doctrine of parliamentary sovereignty over religion. It was rooted in his conviction that an English parliament represented the nation as a whole, and that all true English subjects were by definition members of the Church of England. For all his firm loyalty to his queen, this was a subversive sentiment. It came alarmingly close to the accusation allegedly made by Thomas More: that an English parliament was taking on itself the right to decide how God ought to govern his Church, and so over-reaching its powers like the proverbial Canute. When Parliament defied royal authority during the Civil War, royalists asked: would the next step be to decide on the existence of God by majority vote?

In fact, the tug of war between royal and parliamentary authority over the Church was never decisively resolved. Instead, the 'Glorious Revolution' of 1688–9 changed its terms, by setting in motion a decisive shift of power away from monarchs: not only to parliaments, but also to the ministers drawn from those parliaments, who increasingly exercised 'royal' powers on their monarchs' behalf. The two sets of powers have fared differently. Parliament's legal authority over English religion was by now unchallenged: the two Convocations, the English Church's own ancient synods, which had been subordinate to Parliament since 1532, ceased holding substantive meetings at all after 1717. But Parliament's role looked increasingly odd. After the parliaments of Scotland and Ireland were merged into that of England in 1707 and 1801 respectively, and especially after the admission of Catholics and of Protestants outside the established churches to the British Parliament in 1828–9, Hooker's fiction that Parliament spoke for the Church of

England looked threadbare. During the nineteenth century, parliamentarians – like medieval popes before them – grew increasingly wary of attempting to exercise the authority they formally claimed. In 1919 this situation was somewhat regularized when Parliament delegated its powers over the English Church to a newly formed Church Assembly, subsequently re-formed in 1970 as the General Synod.

Even so, these bodies remain, in law, dependencies of Parliament, which ratifies and can in principle overrule their decisions. Notoriously, it did so in 1928, when the House of Commons blocked proposed (rather modest) revisions to the Book of Common Prayer – Conservative MPs overruling bishops and clergy on points of liturgy in a very Elizabethan manner. In 2012, when legislation to permit women bishops narrowly failed to reach the necessary supermajority in General Synod, the resulting outrage sparked serious talk of Parliament overturning the decision. When the prime minister urged the Synod to 'get with the programme' and publicly mused about giving it 'a sharp prod', he was doing more than offering his private opinion as an Anglican layman. In 2014 the Synod obediently voted through a revised proposal. Parliamentary authority over the English Church, then, is sleeping but not dead. It does not need to be openly exercised for it to exert a gravitational pull.

Yet the authority claimed directly for the monarch under the Royal Supremacy also remains enormously important; it is merely no longer vested in the monarch personally. 'Royal prerogative' powers, exercised on the monarch's behalf by the prime minister, are a central part of Britain's make-shift constitution. In church matters, this chiefly affects the very many senior posts, including all bishoprics, which are 'Crown appointments'. For centuries these appointments remained under direct government control. That has been progressively weakened, but even now, bishops are formally appointed by the prime minister on behalf of the Crown. Until 2007 – astonishingly – the prime minister had a genuine choice of candidates for bishoprics, and while the Church committees could indicate who they favoured, a prime minister could overrule this and impose his or her own favoured candidate, as Margaret Thatcher did in 1987.

That last vestige of nakedly political control over the Church has now been abandoned, but the vast system of 'patronage' which governs the Church of England's appointments at every level remains in place. 'Crown appointments' are now more or less controlled by the Church's own institutions, which give a voice to its faux-democratic Synod. But even now most English parish priests are 'presented' for appointment by 'patrons' who are often local landowners, or corporate entities like cathedrals or colleges. This system is much less corrupt than in the days when it provided the narrative spine of many a nineteenth-century novel, but it still ensures that the congregations that constitute (and fund) the Church of England have a remarkably muted voice in their own pastoral care and governance. This is a direct legacy of the Tudor Reformation. The system has medieval roots, but it was when swathes of church lands were given into secular hands in the reigns of Henry VIII and Edward VI that the rights of patronage associated with those lands were transferred to their new, lay owners. There was no shred of theological justification for this, but those rights were property in the eyes of the law, and the new owners were unwilling to renounce them – not least because they were often able to use them to cream off substantial amounts of church income. Even at the time this looked indefensibly corrupt.

In 1546 a future bishop of Ely, Richard Cox, prophesied that 'our posterity will wonder at us' for having permitted 'the wolves of the world' to subject the Church's ministry to 'the greediness of a few'. Indeed we will. Over the centuries this stranglehold has been loosened, chiefly because landed wealth no longer dominates England as it once did, but the old lines of control persist. It was no accident that for many generations the Tory party, which represented England's landed interest, was also the political face of Anglicanism.

If the legal and structural legacy of the Tudor Reformation is pervasive in the Church of England, another set of legacies is less visible but, at least in modern terms, more consequential. The Tudor Reformation transformed the relations between the peoples of the islands of Great Britain and Ireland. We have already noticed how the Reformation brought Wales fully into the structure of the English state. One result was that, until the creation of the Welsh Office as a government department in 1965, Wales as such had no distinct legal existence.

Ireland was harder to digest. Although the island was formally a lordship of the English Crown in medieval times, English control over large parts of it was nominal at best. The early Tudors were already discontented with this status quo, but Henry VIII's break with Rome made it intolerable – partly because his opponents in Ireland were quick to claim the mantle of papal loyalism; partly because the English lordship was of old based on a papal grant. In 1541 an Irish parliament declared Ireland to be a kingdom in its own right, with Henry VIII as its king. This set in motion over 60 years of intermittent but accelerating conflict as successive English regimes tried to turn their grand claims into reality, and as many of the Irish became entrenched in their resentment of the English and the Protestant religion they were trying to impose. Finally, the gruelling Nine Years' War of 1593–1603 ended with England establishing genuine military control over the entire island for the first time ever.

One of the many prices of this victory was the long-term alienation of most of Ireland from both Englishness and Protestantism. England's solution was to import some instant Protestants, planting large numbers of Scottish and English settlers in Ulster, hitherto the heartland of anti-English resistance. In this fashion an inter-island conflict also became an intra-island one, as it has remained down to the present. Successive English and British governments have, between then and now, tried a great many solutions to the 'Irish question' that they created in the wake of the Reformation. Often – from the panic sparked by the Irish rebellion of 1641, through the Catholic emancipation crisis of the early nineteenth century and the late Victorian confrontations over Home Rule, to the Irish border conundrum of the late 2010s – the 'question' has threatened to break British politics apart. There is a certain rough justice in this. The problems are, deep down, of the British state's creation. Yet the British population at large remains surprisingly ignorant of the tangled history that connects the two islands, broadly preferring – like successive generations of British politicians – not to think about Ireland until it forces itself on to their attention. Which, as a result, it periodically does.

Scotland's story is a considerably happier one, but is equally in the Reformation's shadow. Throughout the late medieval period, the kingdom of Scotland had guarded its hard-won independence against repeated English attempts at conquest, and had done so in part by an enduring strategic alliance with France against the shared 'auld enemy'. At first the Tudor Reformation seemed likely only to reinforce this pattern. Henry VIII's gauche attempts to persuade the Scots to join him in schism had no purchase in a kingdom which was served very well by the status quo. Another bloody, failed attempt at conquest in 1544–50 hardly helped. And then, in 1559–60, everything suddenly changed. France was threatening to turn from Scotland's ally into its overlord. The Scottish queen, Mary, was married to the French King Francis II; it seemed likely that their sons would be kings of a united realm in which Scotland would be a mere province. Meanwhile, a burgeoning Protestant movement in Scotland – not least among the nobility – was butting up against the Franco-Catholic regime. When a military crackdown in 1559 against Protestant agitators sparked a much larger anti-French rebellion, it was too good an opportunity for the new, Protestant regime of Elizabeth I in England to ignore. A well-judged English military intervention in 1560 secured victory for the rebels without looking like another attempt at conquest, and ended in a diplomatic revolution. Scotland would henceforth be a Protestant state aligned with England against France, an alignment sealed by the deposition of its Catholic queen in 1567, her execution by her English cousin in 1587, and her Protestant son's succession to the English throne in 1603. By then some idealists had dusted off the name of an ancient Roman province and begun to apply it to the new entity that was slowly coming into existence on their shared island: 'Britain'. The Anglo-Scottish alliance that made Britain's existence possible has never been frictionless and has at moments looked fragile, but so far at least it has always endured. And it was unmistakably a product of the Tudor Reformation.

4

Protestant Reformation

Threaded through the grubby politicking of the Tudor Reformation is another story: one of ideas, and of faith, courage and renewal. Whether you are inclined to regard its protagonists as heroes or as fanatics, there is no doubt we are dealing with a different cast of characters. For many people both then and now, this is the 'real' English Reformation, a story which was suppressed at the time and has been deliberately forgotten since, but will not go away.

When Martin Luther's challenge to the Church's hierarchy and doctrines began to spread in the late 1510s, England, with its well-disciplined Church and its long experience of fighting heresy, did not offer particularly fertile soil. But Luther's seeds were scattered there as they were everywhere. Merchants plying the North Sea routes were vectors for the new ideas; a group of German merchants in London were arrested for possession of heretical books in 1526. 'Gospellers' and 'evangelicals' – they were not yet called 'Protestants' – began to be spotted among Londoners too. Another early vector was the international university network. Luther's Latin books were on sale in Oxford as early as 1520. At Christmas 1525, a friar in Cambridge was arrested after preaching a sermon whose acerbic criticism of the Church drew heavily on Luther. By the end of the decade there were networks of curious dabblers in evangelical ideas in both of England's universities.

One remarkable individual went further. In 1523 William Tyndale, who had been schooled at Oxford in Erasmus' idealism, proposed translating the New Testament into English. When he was denied permission, he did it anyway, moved to Germany to have his translation printed in 1525–6, and decisively threw in his lot with the reformers. He became the leader of a small but formidable group of evangelical exiles in the Low Countries, smuggling printed New Testaments and polemical tracts back into England. Book-running networks sprang up. Robert Forman, master of a Cambridge college turned rector of a wealthy London parish, oversaw a distribution web which encompassed the City, both universities, and towns as far west as Bristol. A few daring preachers, spreading out from the universities, began to test what they could get away with.

England's well-oiled anti-heresy machine was not far behind them. Forman's network was cracked in 1528. As Lord Chancellor from 1529 to 1532, Thomas More worked with the bishops in a ruthless clampdown on the new heresies. Preachers were swiftly arrested. Satisfyingly, many of them could be persuaded to recant, but others held firm, and the regime was ready to follow through. Between 1530 and 1533, at least 13 evangelicals were burned as unrepentant heretics, including the most brilliant of Tyndale's colleagues, John Frith, whose conscience would not let him sit safely abroad while his brethren at home suffered. A price was set on Tyndale's own head. Despite his extensive precautions, he was betrayed to the Netherlandish authorities in 1535 and executed the following year.

That should have been the beginning of the end of England's Protestant Reformation. The English Church and state were more than capable of snuffing out such a movement, or at least reducing it to the level of an annoy-ance. But by the time of Tyndale's death everything had changed. Thomas More himself had now been executed for his once-orthodox faith. And Henry VIII's dispute with, and then vendetta against, the pope provided English evangelicals with what seemed a heaven-sent opportunity.

Their alliance with the king was always an awkward one. For a few idealists there was no deal to be done: Tyndale took a stern view of a king trying to claim divine sanction for his adulterous lusts. But for evangelicals who could per-suade themselves that the king's first marriage really was unlawful – and most could, when they tried – the possi-bilities were mouth-watering. Denouncing papal tyranny suddenly became a route, not to the stake, but to royal favour. Many of the people around the king were now evan-gelicals, not least his intended new queen, Anne Boleyn, and his indispensable new minister, Thomas Cromwell, two people who agreed about religion if little else. Henry was staffing his church with men like Thomas Cranmer whose evangelical convictions meant he could rely on them to be as anti-papal as himself. And he was open to diplomatic overtures from the new Lutheran territories of Germany and Scandinavia, as hungry for allies as he was. Evangelicals who were willing to be patient could reasonably hope that the sands were shifting in their favour.

For much of the 1530s, so it seemed. Partial but real victories were chalked up. The monasteries, which to evan-gelicals were vast monuments to clerical self-satisfaction that leached resources from the pious in order to mumble useless prayers for the dead, were suppressed. The net-work of shrines, pilgrimages, relics and indulgences which had lured the faithful into superstition and idolatry were banned and publicly mocked. Fire-breathing gospellers like Hugh Latimer, one of the greatest preachers of his age, were made bishops. And above all – the great achievement, the act which convinced any doubters that the king was fundamentally on God's side – the English Bible was first legalized and then made freely available in every parish. Henry VIII did this because of his touchingly naïve belief that anyone else who read the Bible would discover in it what he had discovered himself – the doctrine of the Royal Supremacy. No matter: for evangelicals, a freely available Bible was almost the sum of all their dreams.

Those dreams were interrupted in 1539–40, when a series of incidents reminded Henry's subjects that he was not, and was not about to become, an evangelical. His personal religion was an eclectic and not entirely coherent mix, built around his conviction of his own God-given authority. In 1539 negotiations with the German Lutherans broke down, provoking Henry into a grumpy legislative reassertion of the traditional doctrines they had tried to persuade him to drop. Cromwell tried to use a new royal marriage in 1540 to relaunch the diplomatic effort, but this match – Henry VIII's fourth – was such a humiliating fiasco that Cromwell lost his head over it. Evangelicals were dismayed, and some fled abroad.

But it was the traditionalists who hoped for a return to Rome who were to be disappointed. During the 1540s, it became clear that Henry would go neither on nor back. Both religious factions scored minor victories. The king firmly stated his opposition to evangelical doctrines of salvation, imposed rather ineffective restrictions on the English Bible and permitted several limited bouts of persecution of evangelicals. He also authorized English-language orders for public and private prayers, ordered a further purge of images in churches and consistently undermined the doctrine of Purgatory.

The decisive change that took place during these confusing years was not in government policy, but among the evangelicals themselves. As they digested the fact that the king was not, and never had been, truly on their side, their doctrines radicalized and their positions hardened. The tipping point came in the summer of 1546. Edward Crome, a veteran preacher with moderate, Lutheran-leaning views, was arrested for a provocative sermon and made a show of defiance. Only after dozens of his suspected supporters were rounded up was he persuaded to make an abject recantation. Some of those supporters, however, turned out to be made of sterner stuff. Abandoning Crome's nuanced positions for more full-throated denunciations of Romish error, a group of them went defiantly to the stake, led by the fiery Lincolnshire gentlewoman Anne Askew. She was celebrated like no English Protestant martyr before her. A swathe of previously moderate gospellers – not least Archbishop Cranmer himself – decided the same year that the time for patience and compromise was over.

And then, just as they had embraced the prophetic certainty of opposition, they were handed the keys to the kingdom. It was not pure political chance that Edward VI's government should end up in the hands of a Protestant clique. The old king had entrusted his young son's education chiefly to evangelicals, since even if he disliked their doctrines, he could at least trust them not to be treacherous agents of the bishop of Rome. And so those who had advocated strategic patience back in the 1530s were vindicated. The nine-year-old king's own Protestant convictions were inchoate but unmistakable. His regimes threw themselves fully behind Archbishop Cranmer's project: to create a fully Reformed Protestant Church in England, now to be modelled less on the pragmatic settlements of Lutheran Germany than on the radical purity of Swiss and southern German cities like Zurich, Strasbourg and Geneva.

If Edward VI had lived, this is what would have happened. The Church of England would have adopted an assertively Protestant confession of faith, structure and order for worship. Cranmer went through two versions of his Book of Common Prayer, in 1549 and 1552, books which steadily weaned the population off traditional practice, ceremonial and doctrine; a third and perhaps fourth edition would have continued this trajectory. Cranmer's idealistic project to renew the English Church's legal structure was blocked by the Duke of Northumberland in 1552, but given another few years, a watered-down version would doubtless have been enacted. Bishops would have been replaced with superintendents. The cathedrals would have disappeared. Cranmer and his allies would have wanted to use the wealth seized from them and from the rest of the Church to train a generation of new Protestant preaching ministers. In fact the government would most likely have swiped the lot. But whether well resourced or not, England would have had a simple and unmistakable Protestant Reformation.

Instead, that moment of possibility would remain a mirage. At first it was replaced by a nightmare: Mary I's accession, England's reconciliation with Rome and an unprecedentedly intense wave of persecution. Almost a thousand English Protestants fled abroad, forming themselves into churches in exile. They prayed for their nation's popish ordeal to end, implausible as that seemed. But they also split bitterly among themselves, a divide which bit most deeply into the exile church in Frankfurt. One party there believed it was a moment to stop the clock, sticking (more or less) to the 1552 Prayer Book and demonstrating their loyalty to the dead king's Reformation. The other party believed it was time, not to pause, but to accelerate: to embrace the spirit of Cranmer's Reformation by surging forward to the destination he had, or should have had, in mind. When this group of zealots were thrown out of Frankfurt, they found refuge in John Calvin's Geneva, and embarked on a series of radical projects: a new translation of the Bible; a new order for worship, based on Calvin's model rather than on Cranmer's; and, for some of them, talk of fomenting rebellion against Catholic rulers. Did the Bible not say that idolatry should be punished by death?

Then Mary too died, and Elizabeth restored a Protestant settlement; but the initial hopes that the Protestants could pick up where they had left off in 1553 were quickly disappointed. True, Elizabeth's 'settlement' of 1559 mostly restored the religious status quo her brother had bequeathed her, albeit with a few alarming compromises. It quickly became clear, however, that she was following her father's example as well: having defined her position, she would not budge from it. As the exiles returned and threw themselves into the work of Reformation, they brought the post-Frankfurt divide back with them. Many of them accepted office in Elizabeth's Church, either content with her settlement or optimistic that they could help to move it in the right direction. Two-thirds of Elizabeth's new bench of bishops were returned exiles. They did secure a handful of victories: in particular, the queen was plainly reluctant to let priests and bishops marry, but if she wanted to staff her church she had no choice. Meanwhile, a minority of the former exiles set their face against the new regime's unacceptable compromises. The wariness was mutual. The Genevans' talk of rebellion left Elizabeth permanently suspicious of anyone associated with that fanatical city.

For the rest of Elizabeth's reign a running battle over the nature of her Reformation ensued, a battle whose outcome appeared to vindicate the rejectionists. The queen consistently blocked any aspirations for further reform, from avowedly trivial symbolic points such as clerical vestments to substantive issues of the English Church's polity and liturgy. There was a moment of hope in 1575 when she appointed a new Archbishop of Canterbury, Edmund Grindal, a former exile who was plainly committed to using his position to press for further reforms. The queen blocked his plans; when he stood up to her, she placed him under house arrest and tried to deprive him of office. The so-called 'Puritans' who aspired to further reforms repeatedly put forward proposals in Parliament and in Convocation, some modest, some weighty. The queen's managers blocked them all. A few despairing Puritans began to trickle into exile again, believing that half a Reformation was no better than none. In 1588–9 one group vented their frustration in a series of scurrilous, wickedly satirical pamphlets aimed at the bishops, under the pseudonym Martin Marprelate. It felt good, but it triggered a crackdown in which a string of dissidents were imprisoned, and a handful executed for sedition.

For these Puritans, then, England's Protestant Reformation was halted almost before it began. Only in 1640–1 did they finally come to power, when the collapse of Charles I's government left him at the mercy of his Parliament. It was the Puritan moment. 'Root and branch' reform of the

Church beckoned. In the event, the king succeeded in dividing his opponents enough to be able to mount a civil war against them, but his eventual defeat should have left the way open. In 1643 a Covenant linking the English Church to its Presbyterian Scottish counterpart was sworn. Bishops were abolished (and for good measure, Archbishop Laud of Canterbury was beheaded). The Prayer Book was banned and replaced with a new, purified order for worship. A formidable assembly of theologians was assembled and charged with drawing up a statement of faith: the result, the Westminster Confession of 1646, remains a touchstone for Presbyterians around the world today.

But once again, the Puritans' dreamed-of Reformation danced out of reach. Outflanked by the radicals whose vision of Reformation was quite distinct (see Chapter 6), shocked by the execution of the king but unable to offer a practical alternative, marginalized in the republic that followed, they were finally left out in the cold when the monarchy and the pre-war Church of England were restored in 1660–2. They now formed 'dissenting' or 'nonconformist' churches: Presbyterians, Congregationalists, even some Baptists. They endured considerable persecution under King Charles II, and then, from 1689 to 1828, a legal regime of 'toleration' which nevertheless systematically discriminated against them. They survived, and indeed from the end of the eighteenth century they were joined by another group of unrepentant Protestants ejected from the Church of England for their refusal to submit their consciences to its laws and processes: the Methodists. Together, these nonconformists have been disproportionately influential communities in English history and also in England's global reach. Yet they never succeeded in their aspiration to define the nation in the way that Presbyterianism, for centuries, defined Scotland. In this sense, England's Protestant Reformation was much imagined, but it never actually happened.

But the purists' perspective is not the only one. While the classic Puritans of the Elizabethan Church were fighting, and losing, their set-piece battles over contentious points of law and worship, another group of Puritans had a different perspective. From their viewpoint, important as those contentious points might be, they were not what the Protestant Reformation was really about. They were only means to an end, and that end was what truly mattered: bringing the pure gospel to England's people, so that souls might be saved and God honoured. The Reformation would not succeed or fail at the level of national politics, but parish by parish and soul by soul. And so a generation of pragmatic, moderate Puritans, many of them impatient for structural reforms, nevertheless reconciled themselves to working within an imperfectly Protestant church, and began the slow work of building a Protestant nation from the ground up.

It did not go well, or so they thought. Their rhetoric is full of the division between the 'godly' minority and the mass of carnal Protestants, 'church-papists' and atheists. They were also widely resented. Moralizing busybodies are easy to dislike; the lines dividing doctrinal self-confidence, obnoxious self-righteousness and rank hypocrisy are thin ones. Both Puritans and anti-Puritans could agree that Puritanism's bid for the nation's soul had failed.

But we should not take them at their word. Puritans were by nature perfectionist, readier to see a glass as one-tenth empty than as nine-tenths full. Their imagined Reformation was an impossible mirage. But their achievements were real. For one thing, the Elizabethan and early Stuart Church's commitment to full-blown Protestantism was undoubted. Elizabeth's third Archbishop of Canterbury, John Whitgift, was a merciless hammer of Puritan dissenters, but also ordered his clergy to study the sermons of the renowned Zurich minister Heinrich Bullinger and stamped out any open defiance of the Calvinist doctrine of predestination. Indeed, predestination – Calvinist Protestantism's most distinctive and divisive doctrine – became the English Church's consensus position, if not quite its unchallenged orthodoxy, during the reigns of Elizabeth and James I. In 1618–19 England even sent delegates to the Synod of Dordt, an international council of Reformed churches summoned to resolve a Dutch dispute over predestination. The other Reformed churches unproblematically recognized their English colleagues as brethren, and the English happily supported the synod's staunch reaffirmation of predestination.

More to the point, the Reformation on the ground was real. It was slow, far slower than Puritans of any kind wanted, but it was relentless. The universities were, by the 1580s, steadily pumping committed Protestant ministers into the Church's bloodstream. Local communities lent their support to the cause. Towns established endowed 'lectureships' to provide themselves with proper Protestant preaching. Even many of the impoverished upland parishes of northern England raised funds to build new chapels and to attract preachers. Handbooks of Protestant devotion written for ordinary believers became bestsellers. And while most people could not afford them, the cheap pamphlets and ballads that passed from hand to hand in post-Reformation England tell their own story. These texts are increasingly suffused with Protestant imagery and assumptions. It is not simply that markers of Catholic thought and identity – saints, sacraments, prayer for the dead – were steadily retreating. Protestant notions of divine providence, Protestant patterns of piety, above all the Protestants' now-ubiquitous English Bible had become pervasive features of English culture. This was now the sea that the English swam in, Puritan and anti-Puritan alike. The Puritans might have lost every battle, but they were quietly winning the war.

Between the Elizabethan settlement and the English Civil War, the Church of England was unapologetically a Reformed Protestant church. It was also much closer to being a truly national Church than it has ever been since. This has left some awkward legacies to later Anglicanism. The fact that many Puritans were driven into nonconformity after the Restoration has given rise to a wholly unjustified myth among Anglicans: that Puritans had been cuckoos in the Church of England's nest since the beginning, and so are not truly a part of Anglicanism's history. The majority of Anglicans are in long-standing denial over their Puritan heritage, reluctant to recognize that these people are part of Anglicanism's story – and fully so, not on sufferance. Meanwhile, a minority strain within Anglicanism is so enthusiastic to claim England's Protestant, Puritan Reformation as its heritage that it asserts that Reformation ought to be normative for Anglicanism, not merely a strand within it.

The plain facts are, first, that the Church of England was once a mainstream Reformed Protestant church; and second, that it is not any more. How it, and the English-speaking world more widely, should deal with that mixed heritage is a story of two books.

The Book of Common Prayer is the more complicated of the two. When Thomas Cranmer introduced its first two editions in 1549 and 1552, it was an alarmingly radical engine of reform. Its form was revolutionary: the old Latin liturgy had been a framework within which lay people could pray their own prayers, but this new English 'common prayer' was intended to be a united voice, in which the minister spoke to the people as much as to God and in which the greatest part of worship was instruction. The outwardly traditional elements of the new liturgy were a *digestif* intended to make two novel features palatable to a largely conservative people: first, the huge slabs of the Bible that comprise the bulk of most of the services; and second, the robustly Protestant theology that its texts taught, especially in the 1552 version. But when the Prayer Book was reimposed by Charles II in 1662, although its text was virtually unchanged from a century earlier, its meaning was reversed. Despite its title, it no longer aspired to national 'common prayer'. It was an instrument of division, not of unity. It was designed to smoke out those who wished to remain part of the national church but could not tolerate this half-reformed liturgy. And of course, its meaning has changed repeatedly in the centuries since, in the many contexts in which it has found a home. Partisans on various sides naturally try to claim one of those historic meanings as authentic and normative. That is not a good reason to believe them.

The second book is of course the English Bible. The English Reformation produced no theologians of European stature, but in Tyndale it did produce a truly great translator. It is a plain fact that he did more than any other individual to shape the modern English language, and that the English Bible he set in motion would become central to English identity for centuries. Tyndale once promised that, if an English Bible could only be set forth freely, he would be willing never to write another word. Henry VIII pursued Tyndale to his death, but he also did as he was asked. He promulgated an authorized version of the Bible in 1539; Elizabeth I followed his example with her own authorized version, the Bishops' Bible, in 1568.

But these royal attempts to seize control of the English biblical tradition were thwarted. The exiles in Geneva in the 1550s produced a new English Bible, eventually printed in 1560. This 'Geneva Bible' had a shaky start, but – in one of his few achievements as archbishop before the queen silenced him – Edmund Grindal succeeded in popularizing it, and it quickly outstripped its official rival. Filled with handy and firmly Protestant annotations to guide readers, it appeared in every format, for the pocket or for the lectern. It seeped into private homes and into England's verbal landscape. When Shakespeare quoted from the Bible, this was the translation he used. When James I set in motion a project to update the English Bible, it was the ubiquitous Geneva version, not the unloved 1568 translation, that he was competing with. The translators who produced the King James Bible in 1611 took a generation or more to win that competition. Their eventual success was partly down to the scholarly care and excellence with which they worked; partly because they very deliberately drew on Tyndale and on their Geneva predecessors, revising rather than re-inventing the text; and partly because they shed Geneva's provocative annotations, making this a Bible for readers in every tradition. They would have been surprised to know that they had created a text that was still read and beloved around the world over four centuries later. But they might conclude that it showed they had faithfully done their duty.

5

Anglican Reformation

The English Reformation gave rise to a phenomenon we call Anglicanism, but not in a simple way. The Anglican 'myth of the English Reformation', which has come in for extensive historical criticism in recent decades, holds that the English Reformation had a distinctively English quality from the beginning which marked it out from its continental counterparts, characterized by moderation, dignity and a desire to find a middle way between competing extremes. The competing Protestant myth sees that 'Anglicanism' as an aberrant latecomer, a mutation that arose in the Church of England during the seventeenth century and is alien to the Reformation. Normally where there are competing myths the truth lies somewhere between them, and so it is in this case, but it is not equidistant. The Protestant myth is quite a lot closer to the mark. Yet Anglicanism does still have Reformation roots to claim.

Some ground-clearing first. The word 'Anglican' was not widely used to describe the distinctive Christianity of the Church of England until after the Restoration of 1660, at the very earliest. The first recorded use of the word was in 1598, by, of all people, King James VI of Scots, when he was reassuring his suspicious Presbyterian subjects that although he did favour bishops in the Scottish Church, he did not mean 'Papistical or Anglican bishopping'. Over the next few decades most of the few recorded uses of the word are, again, by Scots, who employ it to refer specifically to England's bishops. The implication is that England's religion is a sort of decaffeinated Catholicism. Only during and after the Civil War of the 1640s was the word 'Anglican' picked up south of the border, as a means of describing the distinctive religion that the Church of England had practised before the war but which it did no longer. Before that religion was assertively restored in 1660, and especially before it was assaulted in 1640, it is simply anachronistic to refer to 'Anglicanism'. There was no such thing.

What did exist was a Church of England: the *ecclesia Anglicana*. But those terms are deceptively simple. Before the Reformation, 'the Church of England' was a geographical expression. It referred to a portion of the universal Church Catholic which happened to be found in one kingdom, not to any distinctive entity. It was also an expression which did not need to be used very often. The two most common exceptions to that rule are revealing. The first article of Magna Carta guaranteed 'that the Church of England be free'; and Thomas Becket, medieval England's premier homegrown saint, was widely celebrated as a martyr for the liberties of the Church of England. What distinguishes these two cases is that they were about the Church's relationship with the king. For he was one of the few means by which, in practice, the two provinces of Canterbury and York were tied together. For most purposes, despite the Archbishop of Canterbury's nebulous title of primate of all England, the two provinces ran their own affairs. There was no such institution as 'the Church of England'.

It was, therefore, of necessity a king who conjured it into a more tangible existence. At the same time as Henry VIII began to revile the pope merely as 'the bishop of Rome', he and his agents also began to talk constantly of 'the Church of England'. It was a little-noticed stroke of rhetorical genius. The category was traditional and hard to dispute, but it immediately freighted religious questions with nationalism and politics. If offered a choice between loyalty to the Church of England or to the Church of Rome, only a traitor would even hesitate. Traditionalists arrested during the 1530s might be asked who they believed was the head, under Christ, of the Church of England; to give any answer other than the king of England sounded not like the universal faith, but like treason. 'The Church of England' was becoming what it would remain: an institution whose name asserted that it comprised the entire nation, even though it did not do so then and never has since.

Was there anything 'Anglican' in the modern sense about these Henrician beginnings? Anglicans, understandably sensitive to the jibe that their Church is an accidental by-product of a king's lusts, have generally not wanted to play up their debt to Henry VIII, but it is there. The link is not so much to the doctrinal and ceremonial hotchpotch of Henry's Church as to the rhetoric that he wove about his incoherent religious settlement, a rhetoric that many of his subjects found deeply compelling, remaining loyal to it long after his death. Henry VIII was the true begetter of that most Anglican of ideas: the *via media*. He consistently claimed to be finding a moderate middle way between the extremists who beset England on every side, calling each other 'papist' and 'heretic' while he, their divinely anointed king, was simply trying to unite them around God's truth. In 1545, at the end of an abrasive parliamentary session, the king addressed both houses in these terms, begging them to be united in brotherly love: he wept as he made the appeal, and so, according to our witnesses, did most of his audience.

In fact Henry's ill-defined 'middle way' was not what we would nowadays call 'moderate'. If his speech to Parliament in 1545 was one kind of 'moderation', another had been on show five years earlier, on 30 June 1540, when the king had arranged for three papal loyalists to be hanged, drawn and quartered for treason alongside three evangelicals who were being burned for heresy. That example reminds us that 'moderation' is a word whose meaning has shifted over the centuries. In the Tudor age it referred to an active process, done forcefully by one person to another, meaning something like 'disciplining' or 'bridling', a sense which now survives chiefly in the title 'moderator' given to certain officials.

Once Henry VIII was dead, nobody else was interested in mixing his particular religious cocktail, but some of his subjects had developed a taste for some of its ingredients, not least this notion of vigorous moderation. In 1540 Archbishop Cranmer had written a preface to the regime's official Bible which described two parallel dangers for England's incipient Reformation: that foot-dragging papists would hold it back; and that overeager zealots would race too far ahead and lose their way. Keeping the country together, preferably in lockstep, was his priority. The same principle informed the Book of Common Prayer, a text suffused with talk of national unity, spurring laggards and bridling enthusiasts.

Of course, all this moderation-talk should not be taken at face value. Any position can be made to appear like a *via media* if you choose your extremes carefully enough. The regimes of Henry VIII and, even more, Edward VI exuded quiet reasonableness in order to distract attention from the revolutionary change their commissars were enforcing. But it was not merely a smokescreen. The Reformation was genuinely pregnant with radical possibilities, which Cranmer and his allies were determined to abort. Edward VI's regime executed no Catholics for loyalty to the pope (although plenty were executed for rebellion), but it did burn two Protestant radicals for heresy, and virtually all of its leading propagandists wrote works against Protestant radicalism of one kind or another. The zealots straining at the leash were sometimes useful outriders for the regime, but those who ventured too far ahead were liable to be brought back firmly into line. John Hooper, who had spent the early 1540s in exile in Zurich, become one of the Edwardian Reformation's most forceful defenders, and was given the strategic twin bishoprics of Worcester and Gloucester. But when he refused to wear traditional vestments for his consecration as a bishop, seeing them as popish rags redolent of superstition, he was thrown in prison until he agreed, reluctantly, to conform. This was not because Cranmer and his allies placed any particular value in the vestments themselves. What they valued was discipline and unity. They had little patience with idealists who listened to their individual consciences above the collective voice of the English Church.

This much was simple pragmatism. But there was also a more principled side to the story. By the mid-sixteenth century, Europe was well on the way to dividing into polarized, sharply defined Protestant and Catholic camps, but the process was not yet complete and plenty of earnest and conscientious Christians deeply regretted it. Many still hoped to find a middle way of some kind: to assimilate Luther and his evangelical followers into Catholic Christendom like so many reformers before them. In the 1540s the

Prince-Archbishop of Cologne, Hermann von Wied, became a hero for these idealistic centrists, drawing eirenic Protestants into a doomed attempt to walk the knife-edge of evangelical Catholic reform in his strategically pivotal diocese. In the early 1550s, drawing in part on von Wied's work, Archbishop Hamilton of St Andrews embarked on a Catholic Reformation of this kind in Scotland. There were parallel efforts in Sweden, in Hungary and even in France.

Cranmer himself admired von Wied; others in England took this movement more to heart. Under Edward VI, muted voices can be heard yearning to return, not to Rome, but to what loyal nostalgia saw as the 'moderate' Reformation of Henry VIII. Such people had swallowed the old king's anti-papalism and his fastidious dislike of 'superstition'. John Proctor, whom we met in Chapter 2 coining the word 'Deformation', openly opposed both Edward VI's Reformation and the pope's 'false forged power'. He deplored how England had, in former generations, been 'trained in worshipping stocks and stones', and celebrated the advent of the English Bible, 'that comfortable treasure of God's sweet word'. The distinguished Cambridge theologian John Redman likewise lambasted 'popish superstitions' while seeing the Edwardian reformers themselves as 'worse than pagans and infidels'. Doctrinally incoherent as Henry VIII's Reformation might have been, some at least of his subjects found it emotionally appealing.

Under Edward VI, these latter-day Henricians were a curiosity. Under Mary I, they were an irrelevance, accepting reconciliation with Rome with a pang of regret that the moderate Reformation they had dreamed of was now impossible. Or so they thought. It was in 1558–9 that the moment arrived for these reluctant reformers. Now they had a queen who was at least partly on their side. Elizabeth I was a Protestant, but of a distinct, rather old-fashioned kind. Idiosyncrasies on her father's scale were impossible by this time, since the religious battle lines were by now much more sharply drawn, but she did her best; it was most unusual for a Protestant queen to dislike married clergy, cherish choral music and keep a crucifix in her private chapel. Her adamantine refusal to allow any further changes to her religious 'settlement' after 1558–9 was in large part a political decision: she was painfully conscious of the risks of alienating her more conservative subjects; she was equally aware that her 'Puritan' subjects would take a mile if they were given an inch; and the more she was pressed to give ground, the less inclined she was to do so. But it was also a matter of personal taste. A dignified, ceremonial form of Protestantism, which liturgically celebrated the nation's unity rather than preaching up a storm of discordant opinions, was to her personal taste. And because she was queen, she could and did impose her personal taste on the nation.

Most of her subjects conformed to this settlement, some contentedly, some chafing at it in some way or other. A few, however, began to show positive enthusiasm for it. This emerging movement had three strands. There was a ritual, devotional and aesthetic strand, nurtured in the cathedrals and a handful of other unusual churches – above all, in Westminster Abbey, England's most anomalous church: a cathedral with no bishop, a church with no parish, a free-floating entity answerable only to the Crown. These churches served as reservoirs in which ceremonial religion could persist even as it drained away from the rest of England. Choral music flourished in them, and if many of the composers were Catholics, what did that matter? The queen's insistence on the legitimacy of these practices, and her stout defence of the Prayer Book in particular, gave courage to others who cherished them. By the end of the century, a new generation of preachers, many of whom had come up through Westminster or at the Chapel Royal, were defending these practices, not only as legitimate, but as pious and edifying, certainly more so than the austere minimalism of Reformed Protestantism. The prince among these was Lancelot Andrewes, dean of Westminster from 1601, one of the finest preachers of his generation, with a gift for finding rich layers of spiritual nourishment in traditional practice.

A second strand centred on the perennially explosive issues of jurisdiction and polity. By the 1570s, Puritan doubts about bishops had evolved into demands that the office be abolished altogether, in favour of a more egalitarian, presbyterian structure. In response, the establishment's defence of the status quo hardened. Instead of merely arguing that episcopacy (government by bishops) was legitimate, the regime's publicists began to advance positive arguments in its favour. Some even began to argue – as Richard Bancroft, a future Archbishop of Canterbury, did in 1589 – that episcopacy was not merely the best structure of church government, but was actually mandated by God's law.

In later centuries this would become an Anglican orthodoxy, but for now it was an outlier. Richard Hooker, the most enduringly influential thinker in this tradition, had a more modest view. Hooker spent the decade before his death in 1600 writing his vast *Laws of Ecclesiastical Polity*, the closest thing modern Anglicanism has to a theological foundation text. It is characteristic of what Anglicanism would become that Hooker's focus was, as his title suggests, law and structure rather than systematic theology.

Among many other things, he argued that episcopacy was the best possible system of church government – but not, he was careful to add, the only legitimate one. He had no desire to unchurch his bishopless brethren elsewhere in the Protestant world. For Hooker, unlike many of his later admirers, was still self-consciously a Reformed Protestant, and an admirer of the church of Zurich in particular. He insisted that Elizabeth's Church stood squarely in that tradition, a tradition that the Puritans were wrongly claiming exclusively for themselves.

The third strand of this 'avant-garde conformism', as one historian calls it, was more explicitly theological, and centred on Reformed Protestantism's great doctrinal shibboleth: Calvinist predestination. As we saw in the last chapter, predestination was more or less the doctrinal consensus of the English Church in the years around 1600, but that consensus was never fully settled or stable. Predestinarians continued to spar about the precise extent and definition of the doctrine. Theologians such as the great William Perkins, the first English Protestant writer to find a truly international readership, devoted enormous effort to resolving the pastoral problems that the doctrine produced, and no matter how subtle and humane his solutions might be, his efforts testify to a persistent problem. In every country where Calvinist predestination became an orthodoxy, it also provoked opposition from within the Calvinist fold. The Church of England was, in this respect, at one with its sister Reformed churches.

What brought English anti-predestinarians out into the open was, ironically enough, the Synod of Dordt, the international Calvinist synod of 1618–19, which – with explicit English backing – reaffirmed a stiff doctrine of predestination and stamped down an insurgent Dutch anti-predestinarian movement. It should have been a moment of Calvinist triumph. Instead, the publicity it gave to the dispute awakened English anti-predestinarians from a 'dead sleep', and made the synod's hardline doctrines look like a contentious (and foreign) partisan position rather than a settled orthodoxy. The doctrine had always felt morally counter-intuitive. That feeling now became the glue which brought ceremonialism and episcopalianism together into a newly energized movement to celebrate the distinctive heritage of the Church of England. The fiercest partisan of the new unorthodoxy was the future bishop Richard Montague, who in an anti-predestinarian tract in 1624 did something no English Protestant had dared before: to use the old notion of the English Church as 'moderate' to claim that it stood halfway between Geneva and Rome. It was as shocking as claiming to position yourself halfway between good and evil.

The litmus-test question was this: when was the Church of England founded? Staunch Protestants were queasy about asserting any continuity between their Church and the medieval past, believing that the pre-Reformation Church was a 'synagogue of Satan' and that the flame of true Christianity in that era had been kept burning by a motley band of persecuted heretics and dissidents. It was a tricky argument to make, and not only because of the evident institutional continuity between the pre- and post-Reformation Churches – medieval laws, structures, finances and even buildings had been updated piecemeal and partially rather than being dismantled and refounded. Worse, the monarchy itself was deeply and unavoidably invested in the notion of unbroken, centuries-long precedent. If all those kings and queens had been mere dupes or co-conspirators of Antichrist, what became of the ancient majesty of the English Crown? Better by far to take Richard Hooker's line: that the medieval Church was a true Christian Church that had stumbled into error, but which merely needed to be reformed, not overthrown. Perhaps parts of its heritage could even be reclaimed and cherished.

Which is to say: it is no accident that this pattern of thinking was particularly appealing to kings, queens and their most ardent supporters. The ceremonial revival was predominantly a movement by clergymen, for clergymen, but it did win over some prominent laypeople. By far the most important was James I's son, who in 1625 became King Charles I. James had been intrigued by the ceremonialists. Charles was entranced by them, and became a true believer. He packed them steadily on to the bishops' bench. In particular, he made the committed, combative ceremonialist William Laud bishop of London and then, from 1633, Archbishop of Canterbury. The 1630s are known to historians as the era of 'Laudianism'.

What that era meant depended on who you were. For Laud's allies, it was a flowering of theological and liturgical creativity after the arid years of Calvinist dominance. Rich spiritual explorations within traditionalism were undertaken by figures as diverse as John Cosin, the future bishop of Durham; George Herbert, the priest-poet of Wiltshire; and Nicholas Ferrar, the founder of a religious community at Little Gidding, Cambridgeshire, which had a tang of monasticism about it. The legacy of these 'Caroline divines' has been treasured within Anglicanism ever since, and rightly so. The other side of Laud's counter-revolution is not now so widely celebrated. He demanded and enforced strict ritual conformity. In particular, he insisted that communion tables should be returned to the eastern end of church buildings, like Catholic altars, and that they should be set about with rails, cutting them off from the people. This pattern is now normal in most Anglican churches worldwide, but in its time, to place tables 'altarwise' felt as if the Reformation itself was being undone. Yet neither Laud nor the king would brook resistance. The Laudian 'persecution' should not be overstated – the anti-Laudians' careers were ended, not their lives, although there were certainly imprisonments, and in one notorious case in 1637 three outspoken critics had their ears cut off. Even so, if this was 'moderation', it was very much of Henry VIII's kind.

Had Charles and Laud not overreached, they might have succeeded. A great many English people disliked these innovations, but others welcomed them, and there was a decades-long habit of obedience. It was the attempt to impose similar innovations on Scotland, home to a much more purist Calvinist Church and to a much less tame political culture, that was foolhardy. Charles ignored warnings until Scotland erupted into open revolt in 1637, setting in motion a chain of events which saw England, too, descending into civil war. Eventually the victorious parliamentarians abolished bishops and banned the Book of Common Prayer, and ultimately the parliamentary army put the Church of England's Supreme Governor on trial and cut off his head.

This catastrophe was, in fact, the making of Anglicanism. The anti-Laudian reaction had been fierce, but had revealed that a great many English people now identified, if not with Laud's full slate of changes, at least with the Book of Common Prayer that Puritans so reviled. The book was banned in 1645, but the law, like many others from this chaotic period, was scarcely enforced. The bishops were deprived of office, but those who chose to remain in England were allowed to operate more or less freely, and ordained enormous numbers of priests during the civil war and republican years. The era of disestablishment was certainly hard for these traditionalist Prayer Book Protestants, but it did give them two gifts. First, freedom: no longer subject to suspicious episcopal discipline and to the straitjacket of national 'common prayer', clerics like Jeremy Taylor could experiment with liturgy and with their own tradition as never before. Second, identity: because they were no longer merely 'the Church of England', they were compelled to find new ways to think of themselves. What better term than the jibe made by their martyred king's father? They were 'Anglicans'.

So the seeds of Anglicanism had been sown in the English Reformation from the beginning, and had germinated periodically through the sixteenth and early seventeenth centuries; but always in the shade of larger and better-established growths. It was the ceremonialist revival of the 1620s and 1630s, immediately followed by the years of exile in the 1640s and 1650s, that turned what had been a minor theme into a dominant force, a new kind of Protestantism rooted in England's peculiar conditions. When, against all expectations, the monarchy was restored in 1660, King Charles II also restored an entity which still wore the name of 'the Church of England'. It was not true. It was, instead, the Anglican Church, in something like the modern sense of the word. And that, despite or even because of its belief that it could trace an unbroken history back to Augustine of Canterbury in the sixth century, was something new.

6

Radical Reformation

Our final narrative of England's Reformations is the most problematic, the most fragmented and maybe the most consequential. This is not a unified story. Its actors would not have recognized one another as brethren and the connections between them are often speculative at best. They are the assorted debris of the Reformation, pieces flung out because they did not or would not fit, and were in their own times generally treated as fringe extremists or irrelevant curiosities. Only in retrospect do they add up to something.

They also challenge the English Reformation's standard chronology, which runs conventionally from Henry VIII's reign to the late sixteenth or mid-seventeenth century. For this story begins with the so-called 'Lollards', a loose movement of religious dissent endemic in parts of fifteenth- and early sixteenth-century England, deriving ultimately from the unorthodox fourteenth-century Oxford theologian John Wyclif. Their importance has often been exaggerated, whether by their contemporaries' hypersensitivity towards heresy, or by later Protestants' eagerness to confect a medieval lineage for themselves. It is very tempting to discern Lollard involvement in, for example, the great Peasants' Revolt of 1381, one of whose leaders, the renegade priest John Ball, famously preached that 'from the beginning all men by nature were created alike', and that divisions of wealth and status were a 'yoke of bondage' to be thrown off. Well, perhaps. Regardless, he did not leave much of a legacy behind him.

The later Lollards, from the 1420s onwards, preached neither John Ball's revolution nor John Wyclif's sophisticated, idealistic critique of orthodox religion. They held on stubbornly, a persistent presence in some English towns (London, Bristol, Coventry) and regions (Buckinghamshire, Essex, Kent, Oxfordshire), but were no longer advancing. They apparently had only one unvarying, positive doctrine: the conviction that the Bible in English should be freely available. Beyond that their beliefs were a series of denials. They generally rejected any notion that a person, place or object could be sacred. So they despised priests as oppressive hypocrites; ridiculed sacraments – sometimes all of them – as meaningless; reviled images, relics, rites and sometimes even church buildings as mere monuments to superstition; and were quite ready to deride traditional Christian doctrines linked to those monuments. Wyclif had criticized the doctrine of transubstantiation, the miracle by which Christ's body and blood were made physically present in the mass, in subtle philosophical terms. The later Lollards, although claiming Wyclif as their inspiration, used vicious mockery instead. In an age which revered the Virgin Mary, they derided her with crude innuendos. Sometimes this kind of talk seemed to imply deep questions about the nature of Jesus Christ's humanity, but they were not trying to raise profound theological questions. They were kicking against the pricks.

This century-long malcontented rumble posed no very serious threat to the Church. Lollard numbers are impossible to estimate, but there were not many of them, even in their strongholds. Most of them continued to attend their parish churches, while also meeting discreetly in one another's homes to read and pray and argue. They had no churches, no ministers, and no structures aside from informal networks which circulated forbidden books. They had no more than a handful of sympathizers among the gentry and the clergy. Steely anti-heresy legislation passed in 1401 helped to keep them on the margins. Enforcement was sporadic; periodically, a bishop might lead an anti-heresy drive for a few months, often as a means of demonstrating to his orthodox flock that he meant business. Such purges usually consisted of rounding up the usual suspects, most of whom would be induced to recant their errors, with only a handful being persistent or unlucky enough to be executed. Lollardy was, from the hierarchy's perspective, like a persistent infestation of fleas: a nuisance that stubbornly defied extermination, but not a mortal danger.

English Protestants have often claimed the Lollards as their ancestors, but in fact the Lollards seem to have done little to prepare the way. Few of the first leaders of English evangelicalism had any discernible debt to the Lollards. The evangelicals' core message was overwhelmingly about faith and the nature of salvation, a message which derived entirely from Martin Luther's movement and owed nothing at all to Lollardy. Lollards generally recognized those evangelicals as brethren, listening eagerly to their preachers and buying their books. By the middle of the sixteenth century – at the latest – Lollardy had simply vanished into the burgeoning Protestant movement, whose critique of traditional religion was far suppler and more coherent, and whose leaders were, unlike most Lollards, ready to seal their faith with their blood.

But Lollardy still had a part to play. In the first, fragile years of English evangelicalism, long-standing Lollard networks were a ready-made audience, and were invaluable vectors for the transmission of forbidden books. More significantly, English evangelicals, who were painfully aware that their movement looked like a heretical innovation rather than ancient Christian truth, were keen to seize any form of historical legitimacy they could. Claiming the Lollard heritage for themselves was an obvious gambit. Lollards had never made use of the printing press, but from the late 1520s onwards, evangelicals were publishing old Lollard texts as proof that they had a tradition behind them. This effort continued long after the last people we can plainly identify as Lollards vanished from the record. The English Reformation's great historian John Foxe was an early enthusiast for Lollardy, and his research assembled a good deal of what we now know about the movement. For him, the Lollards were part of a thin but unbroken thread of faithful English Christianity running through the dark centuries of papal tyranny.

How far anyone was ever really persuaded by these arguments, we may doubt. But valorizing Lollardy and claiming its heritage had consequences. Lollards and mainstream English Protestants agreed on a great deal – the centrality of the Bible, the critique of the Church and its rites – but not on everything. Lollardy's blunt rejection of any kind of material holiness was much closer to the Reformed, proto-Calvinist Protestantism that became dominant in England from the mid-1540s onwards than it was to the more Lutheran-inflected evangelicalism of the 1530s. Lollard networks may have helped smooth that shift. But many Lollards also held some views that went beyond respectable Protestantism of any kind. So now we need to leave them and turn to the radical themes developing within the Reformation itself – themes which, as we will see, sometimes uncannily echoed the Lollards.

The reforming movement Luther unleashed had been very plural from the beginning. As early as 1521–2 he was openly denouncing the 'fanatics' whose zeal for further reformation had, he believed, led them headlong into dangerous error. This 'Radical Reformation', as historians now call it, came to be associated with two things above all. First, a theological stance: so-called 'Anabaptism', the view that only adults who chose to make a profession of faith might be baptized, and therefore that the Church could only ever be a select group consisting of such individuals rather than a universal body which everyone joined at birth. This idea began to surface during the early 1520s, and the first adult baptisms we know of took place in Zurich in 1525, to the horror of that city's newly minted Protestant establishment. Second, a political stance: the desire to overthrow all existing social and political orders and to inaugurate a new kingdom of the saints, in anticipation of Christ's imminent return. This apocalyptic vision was implicated in the huge wave of popular uprisings in Germany in 1524–5 known as the Peasants' War, and drove the smaller but more intense attempt to create a revolutionary Anabaptist 'kingdom' in the German city of Münster in 1534–5.

Defining radicalism in these terms – as Anabaptist and revolutionary – has two convenient consequences. First, it means that radicalism is sharply distinguished from the respectable, 'magisterial' Protestantism of Luther or Calvin; and second, it means that radicalism was virtually unheard-of in England. Unfortunately, it is becoming increasingly clear that this narrow definition is indefensible. The 'radical' milieu was much more varied and much more deeply intertwined with establishment Protestantism than anyone liked to admit. As to the impact on England, it is true that, until the 1640s, adult baptism as a practice found very few English supporters. When Henry VIII and his evangelical ministers became aware of the presence of a handful of Dutch Anabaptists in England in the 1530s, they pursued them with zeal and executed them without mercy. Despite periodic scares, that particular bogeyman would not appear again in earnest for a century. But other disturbingly radical ideas did persistently bubble up. In what Archbishop Cranmer called 'this world of reformation', what had once been unthinkable became unavoidable.

Three interwoven strands of radical Reformation can be discerned in England during the century following Henry VIII's break with Rome: a perfectionist-mystical strand; a separatist strand; and a utopian strand. Perfectionist-mystical radicalism first surfaced under Edward VI, when the new Protestant establishment was coalescing around a new, hard-edged orthodoxy: the doctrine of predestination, which holds that some of us are eternally predestined to heaven, others to hell, and that all of us are powerless to affect that decree in any way. It is a doctrine which has always struck some people as intuitively repugnant. A small movement of so-called 'Freewillers' – evangelicals who asserted that God permitted them to choose their own eternal fate – sprang up in parts of rural Kent, and elsewhere. During the years of persecution under Queen Mary, the regime actively used this division to stir up trouble among Protestants, but the Freewillers were for the time being outmanoeuvred and discredited by their orthodox brethren. By 1558, the movement had disappeared.

Their ideas did not. We saw in the previous chapter how discontent with predestination helped to spur on the ceremonial revival that would eventually give rise to Anglicanism. Similar processes were at work on the Reformation's other wing. In the 1560s, a Dutch mystical movement known as the Family of Love began to win English adherents. These 'Familists' were not Anabaptists; indeed, like the Lollards before them, they conformed outwardly to the established churches. Instead, they were spiritualists, who treated orthodox Christian doctrine as an allegory for their own mystical quest, a quest whose purpose was not salvation in the conventional Christian sense, but inner union with Christ, or being 'Godded with God'. Unlike the Freewillers of the 1550s, they followed their rejection of predestination through to its full implications. If they were free to choose their own path, surely that must mean they were free to choose moral perfection, regardless of conventional Christian views of original sin? Perhaps, empowered by the Holy Spirit, they could transcend the lumpen business of earthly right and wrong altogether, ascending from the darkness of Law to the light of Grace?

After a wave of panic about Familists in the years around 1580, the sect slowly faded from view, but again their ideas persisted. In the 1590s we hear of English radicals questioning baptism – not advocating adult baptism but arguing that Catholic baptism was irredeemably corrupt; that true Christian baptism had vanished from the world in the dark centuries of popery. Some even concluded that Christians must abandon baptism or any kind of church until God saw fit to send new prophets to renew his people. The last two English people ever to be burned for heresy, in 1612, held views of this kind. One of them believed that he himself was the new John the Baptist.

These were extreme and eccentric positions, but a broader and more troubling variant of 'Familism' would soon emerge. A renowned London preacher named John Everard discovered this tradition during the 1620s, immersing himself in medieval mystical writings and reinterpreting Christianity in spiritualizing terms. The Bible, he now felt, was 'symbolical and figurative', a 'dead letter' which could not be compared to 'the inward word, to wit, the law of God written in our hearts'. A scattering of other zealous Protestants were becoming disenchanted with the English Church's Calvinist consensus and what they felt was its arid moralism. Their inner experiences of assurance and grace persuaded them to transcend crude legalism. During the 1630s, when the Laudian counter-revolution was breaking the Calvinist consensus apart, an increasing number of disillusioned Protestants embraced these radical possibilities. London's underground radical scene was burgeoning. Various splinter groups embraced spiritual union with Christ and jettisoned such relics as conventional prayer or faith in bodily resurrection.

Alarmingly unorthodox as all this may seem, what made it dangerous was that it arose so naturally from mainstream Protestantism. The mystical texts which so enraptured Everard had also been favourites of Martin Luther's; the notion of grace transcending law was one of Luther's signature doctrines. Talk of free forgiveness, a longing for an experience of inner assurance, worries about the corruption of inherited Catholic rites, a wish to rise above the carnal and embrace the spiritual – these were all entirely mainstream Protestantism. Mystics and perfectionists were not a different species from their orthodox neighbours, but a variant easily similar enough to interbreed. That was what made them so frightening.

The same is true of the second radical strand, the separatists. We have already seen how the notion of 'the Church of England', a single, universal church embracing the entire nation, mattered deeply to the English Reformation's sense of itself. Most of the 'Puritans' who yearned for further reformation nevertheless deliberately remained a part of that single, national project. This often involved painful negotiations with their consciences. A recurrent story during the period 1560–1640 is of the Puritan minister who tries to hold down a church position of some kind, who refuses to conform on some point that his conscience cannot swallow – vestments, the sign of the cross in baptism, kneeling to receive communion: there were plenty of tripwires – and who is eventually forced to choose between giving way or being deprived of office. Many such people resigned themselves to a miserable half-life, working perhaps as private tutors, still attending the worship of a church they held to be dangerously corrupt.

These people thought of themselves, rightly, as faithful members of the Church of England, but they were also something else: a brotherhood of the 'godly'. They still sat in the pews alongside their carnal neighbours, but the heart of their religion was elsewhere: in the sermons, 'exercises' and combination lectures they travelled to outside their home parishes, in the informal gatherings with sympathetic ministers where they delved deeper into the mysteries of their faith, in 'godly conference' with one another in private houses. They were a church within a church, and little love was lost between them and their more conformist neighbours.

The final step into open schism was therefore momentous but also natural. Few did it at first, not least because the regime took a very dim view of open separatism. The only foolproof way for an English Protestant to leave the Church of England was to leave England itself. During the 1570s and 1580s the substantial expatriate communities of English merchants in the Netherlands became hosts to separatist congregations modelling what a reformed English Church could be. Most of these communities were Presbyterian: they still wanted an all-embracing national Church, just a different one, free of bishops, those icons of popery and tyranny. There were plenty of Presbyterians in England too, most of them unhappily remaining within the established Church, some eventually taking the dangerous step of withdrawing to form clandestine communities of their own.

Others went further. This movement became known as 'Brownists', although the eponymous Robert Browne, who tried briefly to found a separatist congregation in Norwich in 1581 before launching a more enduring venture in the safety of the Netherlands later the same year, had returned to the bosom of the Church of England by 1585. Brownists, or 'Independents', or 'Congregationalists', aspired not to be a new universal church, but – more modestly, more dangerously – simply to form godly communities of their own, recognizing that the faithful would only ever be a remnant in a reprobate world. They were, in other words, implicitly abandoning the entire notion of a unified Christian society.

These little communities hung on in exile, but while the Dutch were welcoming enough, it was hard to see what their future might be there. They feared they would eventually 'lose our language, and our name, of English'. Then, in the 1610s, a new possibility appeared. England was, after several false starts, beginning to establish colonies on the North American mainland. England's government being what it was, the project was done on the cheap. Settlers who funded their own colonies could buy themselves a remarkable amount of freedom, not least in religion. A group of English Congregationalists in Leiden began negotiating such a deal with King James I. When the *Mayflower* eventually sailed from Plymouth in 1620, half of its hundred passengers were former Dutch exiles. An American colony answered the Congregationalists' dilemma: how to be faithful both to their consciences and their nation? If the solution involved crossing an ocean and settling in an environment so hostile that it killed fully half of the settlers in the first winter, then so be it.

The 'New England' settlement – as it was revealingly called – remained tiny and marginal during the 1620s, but the Laudian reforms of the 1630s pushed a new and much larger wave of English Puritans into separatism and exile. A thousand more Congregationalist 'pilgrims' arrived in Massachusetts in 1630; by 1640 some 20,000 had made the crossing. They would do more than anyone else to set the religious tone of British North America and of the United States as it eventually emerged: fiercely determined in their own piety, conscious of their unique calling, but fully aware that they were a minority in a plural society and a godless world. They preferred to pursue their own perfection rather than wait for others to join them, much less drag others with them.

Theologically, these separatists were, or tried to be, pretty orthodox Protestants. But once they had abandoned the national Church, the line was hard to hold. A great many questions to which Protestants had generally given traditional answers were soon being reopened. Should heresy and blasphemy be treated as crimes? Should Christians accept that warfare could sometimes be just? Could Christians legitimately swear oaths, despite the apparently biblical warnings against the practice? Anyone committed to an all-embracing Christian society with a single, national Church was more or less compelled to answer 'yes' to all of these questions. But once they had abandoned that commitment, morally enticing but politically impractical ideals like toleration and pacifism beckoned. Free of the crushing responsibility to create rules that an entire society might be able to follow, the separatists began exploring new possibilities. Even the old question of infant versus adult baptism reared its head. Why should Congregationalists with scruples about infant baptism not indulge them?

In other words, separatist radicalism and perfectionist-mystical radicalism tended to blur into one another. In 1636–8, the colony at Massachusetts endured a bitter split between a conventionally Calvinist majority and a fringe of dissidents led by the pious, well-educated midwife Anne Hutchinson, who felt that rigid legalism was cramping the gospel's true spirit just as badly in the New World as it had at home. She and her spiritualist followers were ultimately thrown out, but they were welcomed into the neighbouring colony of Providence Plantations – Rhode Island, as it would soon be called – by Roger Williams, who had himself been expelled from Massachusetts in 1636 and was now advocating adult baptism and absolute religious toleration. Denouncing radicalism, it was becoming clear, was the easy part. Preventing it from spreading was a different matter.

And so it was with the third, utopian strand of radicalism: the persistent hunch that Christian society could and should be remade in the light of the gospel. Already in Henry VIII's reign, a few idealists had wondered about using the Royal Supremacy to implement sweeping change: whether that be Thomas Cromwell's relatively modest musings about rationalizing England's bishoprics by re-mapping them on to the counties, so unifying church and secular government, or the wildly implausible scheme conceived by the courtier and financier Clement Armstrong in 1533, which envisaged a comprehensive system of moral surveillance covering every household in England, using the king's newfound spiritual authority to impose a systematic godliness on his subjects.

As the shine came off the evangelicals' alliance with the king during the 1540s, more of them began to dream of projects to build a just commonwealth. Central to most of these concerns was money. The Reformation had made a few individuals very rich, as they had acquired church goods, lands and incomes which the common people had once, naïvely, imagined belonged in some sense to them. In an era in which long-term economic changes were in any case concentrating more wealth in fewer hands, this rankled. Some 'commonwealth' theorists offered relatively modest proposals, focusing on specific laws, chiefly those to do with the enclosure of common land. Others were more sweeping, urging wholesale redistribution of church goods or abolition of the House of Lords. Two things held these disparate projects together: a mood of idealistic moral urgency; and a sustained hostility to the clergy as a caste, from the 'forked caps' (bishops) through the 'purgatory horse-leeches' (monks) to the 'dumb dogs', the ordinary parish priests, drowning in their own 'swinish filthiness'. During Edward VI's reign, as we saw in Chapter 2, this kind of preaching was openly encouraged by the regime – at least until it was implicated in the mass disturbances of the summer of 1549.

In Elizabeth's reign, dangerous talk of this kind was not encouraged. Suppressing it, however, did not make it go away. Sometimes it was blurted out, as in anticlerical spasms like the Martin Marprelate tracts of 1588–9; sometimes it was hidden inside coded critiques. It was, naturally, picked up by our other two groups of radicals. The Church of England of course insisted that its ministers were quite unlike the popish priests who had preceded them: set apart by their godliness, their learning and their orthodoxy, not by sacramental ordination, tonsure and the mumbling of Latin. Therefore – so the argument went – those ministers truly deserved the reverence and obedience which their popish predecessors had falsely usurped. You did not need to be especially radical to be suspicious of this bait-and-switch, merely to notice that not all of the new Protestant ministers were everything they were cracked up to be. Before long, radicals were starting to question the entire notion that a minister needed to be educated, a notion which seemed to give the universities a stranglehold on Christian ministry. Surely it was better to be filled with the Holy Spirit than with human knowledge? Perhaps knowledge, which puffed the educated up with delusions of grandeur, was actually an *obstacle* to true godliness? Perhaps true Christians should go back to Martin Luther's doctrine of the priesthood of all believers, and reject the idea of a separate ministerial caste altogether?

These different, contradictory radical voices do not constitute a single, uniform radical Reformation. But nor were they completely disconnected. They were tied together at both ends of the Reformation period: at the start, in the sense that all of them stood in succession to the Lollards. This is not to claim that a living tradition of Lollard radicalism endured throughout our period, although that is possible: certainly there are intriguing signs that the same villages and even the same families which provided Lollard suspects in the fifteenth century were still hotspots of radical dissent in the seventeenth, and if we cannot quite see how this tradition was transmitted, that is no reason to deny its existence. More substantially, the way that the Protestant mainstream celebrated and memorialized their Lollard predecessors kept Lollard radicalism alive. The Protestant historian John Foxe carefully recorded how Lollards had formed separatist conventicles, argued passionately for justice for the poor, rejected the use of oaths, deplored any kind of established ministry and in some cases – here following Wyclif's lead – embraced pacifism. Foxe, who was generally quick to editorialize, let the bulk of these inflammatory doctrines and practices pass without comment. It is no coincidence that Foxe himself held some disturbingly 'radical' views: in particular, his conviction – highly unusual for the time – that executing anyone, Catholic, Protestant or wild-eyed heretic, for their religious convictions was wrong. For a century and more, radicals eagerly cited the Lollards he recorded as precedents for their own convictions. If the Lollards did shape the English Reformation, this was how.

Nevertheless, until the 1620s all these radicalisms were tiny fringe movements. Even when they found refuge in New England, and won new recruits in the wake of the Laudian counter-revolution of the 1630s, the radicals remained scattered on the margins. What brought them to centre stage was the extraordinary breakdown of the 1640s, when all the themes of England's radical Reformation came together. From the moment when Charles I was forced by military defeat to summon a parliament in 1640, to the point when his son was restored to his vacant throne in 1660, England never had a government that was both willing and able to enforce a uniform religious settlement on the country. And so the radical trends that had been incubating for a century burst into the open. Congregationalist churches mushroomed, as newly liberated Puritans tired of waiting for a national reformation and decided to force the pace. The war of 1642–6 sharpened the mood, as 'middle ways' vanished amid the killing. From 1645 onwards, the reorganized parliamentary army became a vast armed seminary for apocalyptic radicalism. Once the war was over, it was that army which found itself holding the reins of power. To the horror of most of the nation, the radicals were on the march, and no one was going to stop them.

The most obvious consequence of this was the emergence of a swathe of new movements, some of which would become enduring denominations. This was when the Baptists, now one of the largest global Christian families, were born. A minority of Congregationalists were questioning infant baptism; meanwhile, via a quite different route, some perfectionist-mystical sects were also coming to define themselves by the practice of adult baptism. These two communities were deeply suspicious of each other; but shared practice, and the shared enmity of the rest of the country, slowly forced them together, and they uneasily came to profess a shared identity as 'Baptists'. That name was probably given to them by the other truly significant sect to emerge from the post-Civil War years, the Quakers, who took all the radical themes we have been tracking to their logical endpoint. They spiritualized most conventional Christian doctrine; abandoned any conventionally structured church, ministry or sacraments; taught a radical doctrine of human equality; professed pacifism, albeit not as steadily as they later liked to recall; and subordinated all 'religion' to the light of Christ, which they found dwelling inside everyone. From a standing start in the late 1640s, by 1660 there were tens of thousands of Quakers, and their zealous idealism was already spreading across the world.

For each denomination that endured, however, there were dozens of movements that flared up and died away, or were subsumed into the wider culture. These were the years that produced the first-ever campaign for representative democracy (the Levellers); an agrarian commune which hoped to create a world of total equality, virtue and reason by sharing labour and abolishing private property (the Diggers); a mystical movement of self-denial which abandoned any kind of religious practice, individual or collective, while it waited for a new dispensation from God (the Seekers); a revolutionary utopian sect hoping to inaugurate an apocalyptic kingdom of the saints (the Fifth Monarchists); and a great many other groups, real or imagined, dedicated to following particular prophets, to restoring Judaism, to nudism, to moral perfectionism, or to transcending morality altogether. Collectively, their legacy – the true legacy of England's radical Reformation –

is irreducible pluralism. Religious toleration of some kind has been an inescapable fact of English life ever since: whether as a point of principle or as a simple concession to reality. Like it or not, England's religious identity is fractured beyond repair.

Two specific legacies of the 1640–60 period underline the general point. First, the Jews. England's long-established Jewish population had been expelled by royal order in 1291, and for nearly four centuries the practice of Judaism was illegal. The fact that to be English was by definition to be Christian made possible the creation of 'the Church of England' as the Tudors conceived it. By the mid-seventeenth century, the prospering Jewish mercantile community in the Netherlands was creating a commercial incentive for England's ban to be lifted. But the actual decision was made by Oliver Cromwell, England's Lord Protector from 1653 to 1658, a Congregationalist whose personal commitment to toleration was partial (it certainly did not extend to Catholics) but was also real. Like many other radicals, Cromwell believed that Christ's second coming would be preceded by the mass conversion of the Jews to Christianity. Perhaps readmitting Jews to England, as he did in 1656, would help precipitate this? It has not, of course, worked out that way. But it has meant that, ever since, England has been not only a multi-denominational but also a multi-faith country.

A second legacy again touches on Judaism, and on the close ties between the radical Protestant groups in England and the Netherlands. Adam Boreel, the most important leader of the Dutch rationalist group known as the Collegiants, was an Anglophile who had spent a crucial formative period during the 1630s among radical groups in

England. In the 1650s, English Quakers paid a return visit, sending missionaries to Amsterdam and opening channels to the Collegiants. In particular, the Quakers befriended a young Dutch Jew whom the Collegiants had taken in after he had been expelled from his synagogue. This man translated a Quaker tract into Hebrew in the (vain) hope of winning Jewish converts to Quakerism. The Quakers wrote that he was 'very friendly' to their cause, and his own later writings show signs of significant debts to English Quaker criticism of the Bible and of conventional Christianity, although when the Quakers and the Collegiants eventually fell out with one another, their Jewish friend stuck by his Collegiant fellow-countrymen. His name was Baruch Spinoza.

Spinoza is justly famous as the philosophical founding father of modern atheism and rationalism, even though he himself was not an atheist in our sense of the word. Yet his debt to the Protestant radical traditions represented by the Collegiants and the Quakers was profound. His limpid ethical vision did not so much reject traditional Judaism and Christianity as transcend them. In doing so he was true to the radical Reformation traditions of his friends. He is a reminder of a truth that applies not only throughout the English-speaking world but even beyond it: all of us, believer and unbeliever alike, whether we like it or not, are children of one or other of the English Reformations.

Further reading

Collinson, Patrick, *The Religion of Protestants* (Oxford: Oxford University Press, 1982).

Duffy, Eamon, *Fires of Faith: Catholic England under Mary Tudor* (New Haven, CT and London: Yale University Press, 2009).

Duffy, Eamon, *The Stripping of the Altars* (New Haven, CT and London: Yale University Press, 1992, 2nd edn 2005).

Hudson, Anne, *The Premature Reformation* (Oxford: Clarendon Press, 1988).

MacCulloch, Diarmaid, 'The Myth of the English Reformation' in *Journal of British Studies* 30.1 (1991), 1–19.

MacCulloch, Diarmaid, *Thomas Cromwell: A Life* (London: Viking, 2018).

MacCulloch, Diarmaid, *Tudor Church Militant: Edward VI and the Protestant Reformation* (London: Allen Lane, 1999).

Maltby, Judith, *Prayer Book and People in Elizabethan and early Stuart England* (Cambridge: Cambridge University Press, 1998).

Marshall, Peter, *Heretics and Believers: A History of the English Reformation* (New Haven, CT and London: Yale University Press, 2017).

Marshall, Peter and Ryrie, Alec (eds), *The Beginnings of English Protestantism* (Cambridge: Cambridge University Press, 2002).

Overell, M. Anne, *Italian Reform and English Reformations* (Aldershot: Ashgate, 2008).

Ryrie, Alec, *The Age of Reformation: The Tudor and Stewart Realms 1485–1603*, 2nd edn (Abingdon: Routledge, 2017).

Shagan, Ethan, *Popular Politics and the English Reformation* (Cambridge: Cambridge University Press, 2002).

Spurr, John, *The Post-Reformation: Religion, Politics and Society in Britain, 1603–1714* (Harlow: Longman, 2006).

Walsham, Alexandra, *Providence in Early Modern England* (Oxford: Oxford University Press, 1999).

Winship, Michael, *Hot Protestants: A History of Puritanism in England and America* (New Haven, CT and London: Yale University Press, 2019).

Index

Index

Index

Index

Printed and bound by CPI Group (UK) Ltd, Croydon, CR0 4YY

26/03/2025

14648007-0001